D1594439

History of the Tonga Chiefs and Their People in the Monze District of Zambia

American University Studies

Series 21
Regional Studies
Vol. 12

PETER LANG
New York • Washington, D.C./Baltimore • San Francisco
Bern • Frankfurt am Main • Berlin • Vienna • Paris

Santosh C. Saha

History of the Tonga Chiefs and Their People in the Monze District of Zambia

PETER LANG
New York • Washington, D.C./Baltimore • San Francisco
Bern • Frankfurt am Main • Berlin • Vienna • Paris

Library of Congress Cataloging-in-Publication Data

Saha, Santosh C.
   History of the Tonga chiefs and their people in the Monze district of
Zambia / Santosh C. Saha.
     p.   cm. — (American university studies. Series XXI, Regional
studies; vol. 12)
   Includes bibliographical references and index.
   1. Tonga (Zambesi people)—History. 2. Monze District (Zambia)—
History. 3. Monze District (Zambia)—Kings and rulers. 4. Tonga
(Zambesi people)—Missions—Zambia—Monze District (Zambia).
5. Chiefdoms—Zambia—Monze District (Zambia)—History. I. Title.
II. Series.
DT3058.T65S24   1994   968.94—dc20   93-48500
ISBN 0-8204-2451-X   CIP
ISSN 0895-0482

Die Deutsche Bibliothek-CIP-Einheitsaufnahme

Saha, Santosh C.:
History of the Tonga chiefs and their people in the Monze District of Zambia
/ Santosh C. Saha. - New York; Washington, D.C./Baltimore; San Francisco;
Bern; Frankfurt am Main; Berlin; Vienna; Paris: Lang, 1994
  (American university studies: Ser. 21, Regional studies; Vol. 12)
  ISBN 0-8204-2451-X
NE: American university studies / 21

In memory of my late younger brother,
Bholanath,
who appreciated my research endeavors.

ACKNOWLEDGEMENTS

I owe my greatest debt to Mr. Zimba, the Assistant Secretary at Monze Boma (1977–78), without whose support I could not reconstruct the history of the six chiefs around Monze. For verification of my collected information, I relied on, among others, Father Dominic Nchete, the head of the Mazabuka Catholic Mission, and also a brother of Chief Monze. He was very valuable in acting as a reader of my work. I must express my gratitude to those who offered me information and suggestions, and verified sections of the work. They include: the Hon'able Mainza Chona, then Prime Minister of Zambia; the Rev. John J. O'Leary of the Society of Jesus, Lusaka; the Rev. D. Whitehead of the Anglican Church of Lusaka; Bruno Mwiinga, a former student of mine at Monze Night School; and Mr. Atkins and his son of the Anglican Church of Monze, who made available the files on the history of the Anglican Church at Monze. I also met the grand old man of Zambian politics Harry Nkumbula, who came from the southern region, and some other important leaders of the 1970s and as such have narrated some aspects of independence struggle.

TABLE OF CONTENTS

I   INTRODUCTION   1

II FEATURES OF THE MONZE DISTRICT
        AND ITS PEOPLE   11
    Geographic Features   14
    Monze Township   15
    Basic Information Regarding Monze District   20

III HISTORY OF CHIEFS IN MONZE DISTRICT   23
    Chief Monze   25
    Chief Choongo   29
    Chief Mwanza   36
    Chief Siamusonde   38
    Chief Ufwenuka   39
    Chief Chona   40

IV MISSIONARIES IN MONZE   51
    Chikuni Mission   51
    Monze Diocese   59
    Catholic Church at Monze   61
    Anglican Church   62
    St. Kizito Pastoral Church   65
    Seventh-Day Adventist Church   67
    Njola Catholic Church   68

V   SELECTION OF CHIEFS AND
        TRANSFORMATION OF LOCAL AUTHORITY   71
    The Courts   77

VI MARRIAGE PATTERNS AND DIVORCES   79
   Marriage Patterns   79
   Divorce Settlements   80

VII SOCIAL STRUCTURE IN MONZE AREA   87
   Urban Tonga   90
   Whites   90
   Asians   91

VIII LOCAL STORIES   95

IX TYPICAL LIFE CYCLE OF A VILLAGE BOY   101

APPENDIX I   105
   Villages in Chief Monze's Area   105
   Villages in Chief Chona's Area   108
   Villages in Chief Choongo's Area   109
   Villages in Chief Mwanza's Area   111
   Villages in Chief Ufwenuka's Area   112
   Villages in Chief Siamusonde's Area   113

APPENDIX II   115
   SONGS AND DANCES   115

BIBLIOGRAPHY   117

INDEX   123

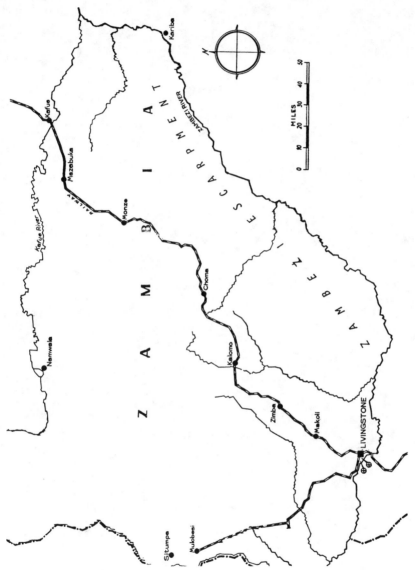

Fig. 1: Map of the Southern Province of Zambia

Chapter I

INTRODUCTION

Geographically, Zambia is a land of gentle undulating plateaux, broken by occasional hills. Along her southern border is the man-made Lake Kariba, part of the hydroelectric system on the famous Zambezi River. There are four major rivers in this Central African country. The largest river, from which the country derived its name, is the Zambezi.

The majority people of Zambia belong to the Bantu-language family. The country has also a fairly small population of Asians, Euroafricans, and Europeans, many of whom are now Zambian citizens. Between 1500 and 1800, the northern, eastern, and western parts of Zambia were settled by Lunda and Luba peoples of Congolese origin, who introduced traditions of chieftainship to Zambia and established several important kingdoms. The Lunda Empire of the powerful Mwata Kazembe appeared in the Luapula Valley in the north in the early eighteenth century. Migrants arrived from the south as well. As people began to flee away from the devastating wars of the "Mfecane" of Shaka the Zulu of South Africa, the Ngoni, forced out of Natal, arrived in the Lwangwa valley in the east of Zambia to settle in the land of the Chewa, Nsenga, and Tumbuka-speaking peoples of the east and the south.[1]

Southern Zambian history has been influenced heavily by the Tonga, although their lack of a centralized kingdom reduced their power considerably. Some eighteenth- and nineteenth-century Tonga sites were found on the Batoka plateau. Extensive ancient village sites were unearthed by archaeologists near Kalomo and Choma towns. A few settlements were traced at Monze, Magoye, and Mazabuka. A strong suggestion has been made by some that the Tonga had lived in these areas for a considerable period of time. Two historians Elizabeth Colson (1962) and B.F. Fagan (1968) have

provided valuable information about the Tonga sites and huts in
the southern province of Zambia. In his book, Andrew Roberts
(1976) informs us that the oldest Tonga settlement known in
Zambia was on the top of the Sebanzi Hill at the Lochinvar Ranch
on the edge of the Kafue flats, not far from the Monze township.
The pottery from the uppermost levels of Sebanze was somewhat
similar to that of the nineteenth century and the modern Tonga
villages in the Kafue river basins. The archaeological evidence
suggests that the Tonga are the direct descendants of the earlier
Iron Age peoples who had lived in southern parts of Zambia over
a thousand years ago. At present the Tonga live in small, rather
amorphous villages without any distinct pattern. Some
characteristic features of the Tonga of Monze area are their shallow
lineages and scattered homesteads rather than consolidated
villages.[2]

The history of the Zambian west is dominated by the Lozi in
Barotseland. Although there may have been remote ties with the
Lunda political tradition, the Lozi state emerged on the fertile
upper Zambezi flood plain as a result of evolution and an extended
period of migration from the north beginning in the late
seventeenth century. By the late eighteenth century, a royal
bureaucracy based on merit supplanted the original titled
aristocracy in Barotseland. The Lozi Kingdom was a remarkably
centralized imperial state, with a graded officialdom and councils,
an extensive tributary system, and corvee labor for military service
and public works.

Europeans first touched parts of Zambia in the early sixteenth
century. A few non-Africans spent a lot of time within the present
borders until the early nineteenth century when Portuguese
entered from the southeast and a little later, Arab traders entered
from the northeast. The Arabs came for ivory and slaves, and
Zambia became a fertile ground for the slave trade. Important

tribes such as the Bemba, Bisa, and Lunda were involved in the human traffic. The Portuguese, coming up the Zambezi River from Mozambique, were interested mostly in trade.

Missionaries did not come until the middle of the nineteenth century and, Dr. David Livingstone was the first of this new breed of Europeans. The missionary interest in Malawi affected Zambia directly. Father Coillard, who visited the Barotseland in 1878 and 1885, laid the ground work for the coming of the British. The Rev. Arnot entered southern and western Zambia, while the Livingstonia Mission of the Free Church of Scotland and the White Fathers entered northern and eastern Zambia. Initially, they met with varying degrees of success in converting the local people.

But it was the strategic interest in the period of so-called British "splendid isolation" that the colonial advances to Zambia were made with all seriousness. Moreover, the Anglo-German naval competition created a sense of urgency in the commercial value of the territory. In 1895, in almost direct response to the German occupation of South West Africa, the British declared their protection over Botswana. This prevented the possibility of the German and Boer alliance that would leave England isolated at the cape route to India. At the same time, the British advance toward Zambia prevented the Portuguese to form a linked stretch of territories between Mozambique in the east and Angola in the west.

The British occupation of Zambia, in the wake of Cecil Rhodes's master plan for the conquest of lands from the "Cape to Cairo," was not sudden; the imperial minded people were inspired by the missionaries to a certain extent. It would perhaps be wrong to suggest that the British colonialists came because the missionaries asked for protection, but at the same time we may conclude that if the missionaries were not there, it would perhaps take longer to get the area under colonial occupation. The explorer, David Livingstone, aroused the British interest in Zambia from 1853 by his speeches and writings, and above all by his discovery of the interior of Zambia including the world famous Victoria Falls.

As a result of the British settlers' advance toward Zambia with the active support of the British South Africa (BSA) Company, the land fell under British control. The BSA Company began to parcel out good lands and allotted them to enterprising white farmers virtually ignoring the rights of the indigenous people. There were 159 farms between Kalomo and Kabwe (Broken Hill) in the early decade of the twentieth century. After 1904 some white farmers lured by the fertile soil and moderate climate arrived in Monze and immediately became engaged in agriculture. Mazabuka, about forty miles north of Monze, was also settled by white farmers. A circular letter preserved at the Mazabuka Boma suggests that the District Commissioner of Mazabuka was asked by the colonial government in Lusaka to prevent friction between the Africans and the whites, because the eviction of the blacks from their farms was not popular. Though, with our present information, no clear conclusion can be drawn with regard to the eviction process and the reaction to it, it is gathered from oral traditions and the general popular belief in the area that the Africans were not allowed to stay near the rail lines. The area adjoining the rail-line in the "maize-belt" was the preserve of the white settlers. Some elderly people in Monze talked of the passive resistance by the Africans, who were evicted from their traditional land holdings.

The European farmers introduced a new type of mixed farming. They enclosed their lands and produced food with the help of the African labor. An elementary style of mixed farming was introduced in the 1920s. The settler-farmers were committed to the fencing of prescribed land in order to protect crops and vegetables and to keep animals within bounds. African farmers used common wood fences, but these were destroyed by insects. Some planted lines of lemon hedges as fences. The white farmers were keen on fencing and they used mostly wire. The fencing itself did not necessarily make a great impact on agriculture. But the lesson was clear: Beasts of burden could be kept safe within bounds, otherwise they would destroy the corn and other fields. The new agricultural method of the Europeans was no different from the "slash and burn system" or the "Chitemene system" of the indigenes. The white farmers borrowed the system of fertilization from their African counterparts. They also cut trees and saplings, piled them together in heaps, and then burned them to make fertilizer.

There appeared with the new type of agriculture a sense of individual ownership of land. The legal concept of ownership was not known to the Africans who believed in the communal ownership of land. This new concept created a break in the tribal sense of community spirit. Thus an European concept was introduced to the Monze area and on the wider scale to Zambia as a whole.

The concept of the large farming gained ground and the prevailing subsistence farming was thought to be inadequate. European immigrants invested in large-scale, highly capitalized farms in the Monze and Mazabuka areas. Nonetheless, indigenous farmers also responded to the market force and produced surplus for sale. Many of them became prosperous village farmers in the Monze-Mazabuka belt. Increased food production and the larger supply of food helped the miners in the south of the Zambezi River. The tradition of small farming was slowly changed and the transformation began to take place.[3]

In her studies of the Plateau Tonga, the noted American historian Elizabeth Colson has noted that the Tonga began to market surplus crops in the 1920s. Several crops, such as maize and groundnut, were sold to the growing markets in the copperbelt, in the north near the border of Zaire. The historian L.H. Gann reports that in the early 1930s, the Tonga, in search of farm profits, began to convert their cattle holdings into agriculturally productive resources. They converted portions of their cattle stock into oxen for drawing plows, sledges and oxcarts, often with the decline in the quality of their breeding herd. It is certain that the farmers in Monze area reconstituted their cattle herds into capital assets. Of the 22,700 plows in the country in 1950, 1,800 were held by the indigenous farmers in the southern area along the line of rail. William Allan submits that the farmers at Pemba near Monze were the first indigenous farmers to utilize manure for the purpose of fertilization. Many farmers specialized in the marketing of agricultural output, which was sent to the urban centers in the 1950s.[4]

Politically, the arrival of the English and South African settlers led to the subordinate status of the Zambians. Means were found by the whites to have a clear control over the majority Africans. When Southern Rhodesia attained self-rule in 1923, attempts were made by the whites to amalgamate the two Rhodesias to enhance political and commercial interests of the white immigrants. The all-European Legislative Council of Northern Rhodesia supported amalgamation and the Central African Federation came into existence in 1953. The creation of the Federation, based in Salisbury, generated political agitation and independence struggle in Zambia. The movement was led first by Harry Nkumbula and then by Kenneth Kaunda. Eventually, Zambia was granted freedom on October 24, 1964. Kenneth Kaunda became its first President and the United National Independence Party became the first ruling political party.[5]

At present Zambia is well known to the rest of Africa, and also to the wider world because of her considerable natural resources, such as copper and other minerals. Zambia's Victoria Falls, or Musi-O-Tunia (the thunder that smokes); the Lwangwa Game Park, the sanctuary of hundreds of elephants, beautiful Lakes Mweru and Kariba put Zambia on the world map. It was the land through which passed the greatest of explorers of Africa, Dr. David Livingstone. He, accompanied by his African associates, passed through the Chief Monze area in the mid-nineteenth century. In the 1970s, the country earned rightly the militant name, the "front line" state on the border of Southern Rhodesia, which was then struggling to attain the majority African rule. Zambia took a tough line against the intransigent Smith regime in Southern Rhodesia, and also against the Portuguese in Mozambique and Angola. In the global arena, Zambia pursued a steadfast policy of nonalignment. She maintained good relations with both China and the Soviet Union, while her relations with the United States remained somewhat strained in the 1970s.

Historians have so far written about the Tonga people of various parts of the Southern Province of Zambia. Elizabeth Colson has vividly described the life, economy, and nature of extended family structures of the Tonga people.[6] My present work is an attempt to describe and analyze the socio-political history of all the chiefs in the Monze area. It takes note of the political landmarks of the people, and their cultural heritage as found through some of their stories. It establishes that the Monze chiefdom was a microcosm through which the tribal life of Zambia could be viewed to identify some of the social ethos of the Tonga people living in Monze District.[7] European missionaries played an important role in the educational and economic development of the area. Hence the study includes the achievements and failures of the white missionaries.

More importantly, the present study is an attempt to record the history that might otherwise not be available from written sources. Based on my field-work and with the help of, among others, a group of Tonga-speaking teachers and students of Tagore Primary School, Monze Government Primary School, and Monze Secondary School, this study records aspects of social, economic and political life of the people in Monze.

Lastly, some of the findings in this book cannot be corroborated in the absence of written records. But the history thus obtained has some relevancy to the people of Zambia, who know their country well but tend to forget the local events as unimportant and yet many national trends are nothing but replicas of the regional affairs.

Endnotes

1   For general history of Zambia, see Brian M. Fagan, *A Short History of Zambia from the Earliest Times Until A.D. 1900* (London: Oxford University Press, 1966); George Kay, *A Social History of Zambia* (London: University of London Press, 1967); Andrew D. Roberts, *A History of Zambia* (New York: African Publishing, 1976).

2   Elizabeth Colson and Max Gluckman, eds., *Seven Tribes of Central Africa* (London: Oxford University Press, 1951); Elizabeth Colson, *Social Organization of the Gwembe Tonga* (Manchester: Manchester University Press, 1960).

3   Richard Hall has offered a sound economic history in his book, *Zambia* (New York: Frederick A. Praeger, 1967). He has made many references to the land of the Tongas.

4   Kenneth R.M. Anthony and Victor C. Uchenda, *Agricultural Change in Mazabuka District* (Stanford: Food Research Institute, 1970); John A. Hellen, *Rural Economic Development in Zambia, 1890–1964* (New York: Humanities Press, 1968); William Allan, "African Land Usage," *Rhodes-Livingstone Journal*, No. 2 (June 1945); Robert H. Bates, *Rural Responses to Industrialization* (New Haven: Yale University Press, 1976).

5 For a good general summary see Irving Kaplan, *Zambia: A Country Study* (Washington, D.C.: The American University, 1979).

6 Elizabeth Colson and T. Scudder, "New Economic Relationships between the Gwembe Valley and the Line of Rail," in David Parkin, ed., *Town and Country in Central and Eastern Africa* (London: Oxford University Press, 1975).

7 Early history of southern regions and also of the Tonga land may be found in W.V. Brelsford, *The Tribes of Northern Rhodesia* (Lusaka: Government Printer, 1957); L.H. Gann, *A History of Northern Rhodesia* (London: Chatto and Windus, 1964); J.P.R. Wallis, ed., *The Zambezi Expedition of David Livingstone* (London: Chatto and Windus, 1956).

Chapter II

FEATURES OF THE MONZE DISTRICT
AND ITS PEOPLE

The Tonga people in the Monze area believe that they always had various types of leaders. In his papers kept at the Livingstone Museum in Livingstone City, Father Dominic Nchete writes that the Monze Chief was a spiritual leader, rain-maker, Mwami, prophet, priest, and mediator between God and human-beings. He was supposed to possess divine power and attribute. We know of this faith also from the local oral traditions, Tonga hyms, oral poetry and prayers. The chief was well known even outside the province for his spiritual influence. He was known as the "Northern Wizard" by the first Dutch settlers in Cape Town.

European settlers had regard only for a person who had some sort of army. As they did not find this among the Tonga, they considered the Tonga people chiefless. European writers referred to the area as chiefless also because the Tonga were not led to the area by any chief as was customary in tribal migrations in Central Africa. There is a consensus among historians and anthropologists that the Tonga in the past did not recognize any political leaders as chiefs.[1] They preferred to live in dispersed households rather than villages, although they were forced to group together in the nineteenth century under the continuing threat of the raiding parties of the Lozi and the Ndebele.

The name "Tonga" was apparently a Shona term meaning "independent," implying a lack of formal political structures. The Tonga shared a closely related dialect, similar matrilineal descent systems, preferential patrilocal residence with dispersed homesteads, and the absence of any formal chiefly institutions to give them separate identities. Many historians argue that there was a lack of a centralized kingdom or large chiefdom and this condition reduced the power of the Tonga considerably in comparison to the Lozi or the Bemba.[2] However, it was the colonial state that convinced the Tonga that they were a tribe. During the British colonial administration which ended in October, 1964, "tribal" administrations were set up by installing chiefs in various parts of the district. The British government appointed tribal officials whom the Tonga significantly called as Government Chiefs.

Local traditions, on the other hand, suggest that there was a powerful chief at Monze before the arrival of the British. The Tonga people tend to confirm that the Chief of Monze was the creation of the people themselves. This was to support the thesis that a great chief like Monze could not be created by administrative measures only. The Tonga inherited a story that the first Monze Chief descended from heaven and called the Tonga people including those living outside the present southern province of Zambia to his chiefdom, near the present-day Monze town.[3] To reinforce their claim that the Tonga people, led by a chief, were different from other migrants, a suggestion has been made that the Tonga in Monze were indigenous inhabitants. Father Dominic Nchete (1960) writes that the Tonga people had always lived in the area. But the historical records demonstrate that Father Nchete's claim is not supportable. The Tonga were migrants to the Monze district.[4]

The earliest written record of the Tonga goes back to 1561 when the Portuguese missionaries, just after the murder of a Jesuit priest called Silveira by the Mwene-Mutapa Ngomo on March 15, 1561, made a cursory mention of the Tonga. Some have suggested that a section of the Tonga people were known several hundred years ago as the Mbara, and that they occupied an area in both north and south of the Kafue River before 1500 A.D. In the map drawn by Bartholomeu Velho in 1561, they are marked in that area. A suggestion has been made to conclude that they also spread across into what is now Zimbabwe and people with Tonga features are still found there. They are called Mbara by the Shona. In 1514 the Portuguese explorer Antonio Fernandes described "Chief's Mbara's country" which, he said, was "a journey of seven days from Monomotapa... there lies a great river between this king and the king of Monomotapa." Fernandes writes, "And from there they bring copper to sell to Monomotapa in ingots like ours and also through the other land." He describes how the Mbara people used to cross the Zambezi River to trade on the northern side of the river. It appears that the Mbara were Tonga people, who traded in ivory and copper with the Arabs.[5]

From the accounts of the oral traditions regarding the chief and the Tonga people several conclusions may be drawn. First, the Tonga people had established a type of chieftainship before the British established the chieftainship in the area. At least, in the mind of the local people, there existed a chief. Traditions suggest that the first chief came to be regarded as the leader of the society because he was a healer. He could cause rain, cure all diseases, and frustrate tricks of the enemies by his communication with supernatural beings. Thus a priest and a prophet turned to be a ruler in Monze. The significance of this claim lies in the fact that Chief Monze commanded respect not only from the local people but also from the neighboring peoples. Second, the local people believe that they had no warrior traditions and had lived in peace for generations before the arrival of the British. Their war drums and dances were for entertainment only.[6]

Tonga languages belonged to the Bantu Botatwe group, which consisted of three separate groups. As Brian M. Fagan notes, languages like Subiya, Totela, and the Leya, are linguistically related to the Tonga. The colonial government began broadcasting in Bemba and Nyanja during World War II, and added Tonga after the war.

Geographic Features

Geographically, the Monze district is mainly an agricultural area. It is composed of some commercial and industrial farms, which are mostly subsistence farms. There is a game reserve in Lochinvar on the banks of the Kafue River. A modern fishing camp has been set up at the extreme end of the Lochinvar Game Park. The park is managed by the central government based in Lusaka.

The Monze district has three main rivers which are only tributaries of the Kafue River. The Magoye River is in the easterly direction of the district. At present a Community Staff Training College stands on the bank of the river. The second river, Namuseba, is in Chief Monze's area. The third river, Mutama, passes through Chief Monze's and Siamusonde's areas.

An escarpment divides Chief Mwanza's and Chief Chona's area. The plateau lies in the commercial farming areas along the rail line, in the whole of the Chief Monze's area, and also parts of Chiefs Choongo and Mwanza's area near the Gwembe District. The Kafue Flats lie west of Chiefs Choongo and Chief Siamusonde's areas. The flats are separated by a high plateau covered by low hills and mounds in the eastern direction.

Recent excavations at Gwisho Hotsprings on the Lochinvar Ranch in the Southern Province have given a clear picture of the people in the area. It has been established that the bushmen hunters lived in family bands, on small camping sites on the edge of the Kafue Flats. Their houses were merely small windbreaks of grass and sticks, and their dead were buried within the settlement. Over thirty skeletons were found from the three Gwisho settlements, which were investigated between 1960 and 1964 by western archaeologists. The hunters subsisted on a wide range of game and fish, as well as wild produce and fruit, available in the acacia woodland. The Lochinvar sites date to the third millennium B.C.

Most of the Monze district is a high altitude country, a part of the Central African Plateau which ranges between 3,000 and 5,000 feet above the sea level. The Gwembe valley was settled by Iron Age communities, who were limited to areas near the sources of perennial water. The Kafue valley near the Lochinvar Game Park now provides grazing land for both domestic and wild animals. The valley has a favorable environment for pastoral living.

The staple crops in the area are bulrush millet, maize, and sorghum, and a range of legumes and cucurbits. Trading in cattle and goats are an important feature of the local economy. Food gathering and hunting are also still significant features of the local economy.

Monze Township

Monze was named after a noted Tonga leader who was the rainmaker at one of the principal rain shrines to which many Tonga belonged. He was associated with the first Jesuit settlement north of the Zambezi River. The original Monze town was about eight miles from the present town. There was a boarding school called Santa Maria. A town of about 4,300 people, it is located on the east side of the rail line in Zambia's Southern Province. In the 1850's, Monze village was reached by many outsiders, including the Mambari traders from the west, Nsenga ivory traders from the east, and the British and other European explorers. In the 1880s the Lozi, led by a rebel named Sikabenga, raided the Chief Monze's village for cattle, and the Tonga called on the Matabele of Zimbabwe for assistance. Sikabenga was killed and other Lozi were routed. King Lewanika of Barotseland in the west used to demand tribute from the Tonga. Chief Chona told me that the Chona area was also attacked before the colonial era, and the chief supplied skins to the invaders, especially to the King of Barotseland as tribute.[7] It appears from the oral traditions that the Chief Monze had cordial relations with the Barotse Chief and as such the Lozi King from Barotseland did not demand any tribute from Chief Monze.

In 1898, Fort Monze, which later housed the colonial security forces, was established by Major Harding of the British South Africa Company Police. The brick-built and well fenced fort was of the first fort in the area. It was in effect the beginning of the white settlement in Monze. At present a Government Police Station is situated near the old fort.[8]

While the African invaders, such as the Ngoni and the Ndebele, came and went, the white presence became permanent in the district. The Jesuit group, led by Father Joseph Moreau, arrived in the area in 1902. The Jesuits were all allowed by the Tonga to set up a mission in Chief Monze's area.[9] Monze has graves of early British administrators in the area. Although David Livingstone of London Missionary Society had passed through the area, the Protestants were slow to arrive.

In 1904, when British Administrator Coryndon established government Bomas at Kafue, Mazabuka, and Kasempa, Monze was placed under the Mazabuka administration. Mazabuka is about forty miles north of present-day Monze. With the advent of the British political domination, taxes were imposed on the Africans in Monze. These were unknown before and naturally there was discontent among the local Tonga people. The hut-tax was introduced in the Monze-Mazabuka area in 1904. It was imposed to raise revenue needed to meet the cost of the British colonial administration. To the annoyance of the local people, the Europeans in the area were not taxed until 1918. Of all the Tonga, the Monze people were the first to be burdened with the taxation. Taxes also had to be paid on goods, such as gold, copper, ivory, livestock, cotton, coffee, etc. If an African could not afford to pay taxes, he was asked to compensate for the tax in work. The official argument was that the taxation was a device to get Africans to work. Many elderly people recalled that there was occasional mild resistance,[10] and the taxation created a hostile feeling against the British.

Along with the white administrators, there came the earnest missionaries, who built a large Catholic Church. The Catholic Diocese of Monze was set up in 1962. Monze is now the residential seat of its Bishop. Bishop Corboy was consecrated on June 24, 1962 at Chikuni, not far from the Monze town. The Consecrator was Father Adam Kozlowieski of Lusaka. The Provincial Father Charles O'Conor came from Dublin, Ireland, for the occasion. Incidentally, Bishop Corboy presented Papal medals to JoJo and Jahaliso, who had gone with Father Moreau to Southern Rhodesia and had returned with him three years later when they, along with others, started the Chikuni Mission under a Musekesi tree.[11]

The Monze Mission Hospital, which earned the status of a district hospital, was initially managed by the Sisters of the Holy Rosary of Killeshandra of Ireland. Among others, Father Daniel Byrne was responsible for the first phase of the construction of the hospital buildings. Monze town became a center of commodity exchange. The National Grain Marketing Board established its provincial headquarters at Monze. The government-owned imposing silos for maize storage stand along the Lusaka-Livingstone highway. The Monze Rural Council has its headquarters on the southern outskirts of the Township. Monze Township Council obtained the Township Council status in April, 1938.

There are three secondary schools in the district. These are the Monze Secondary School, Rusangu Secondary School, and Canisius Secondary School. At Chikuni there is a Teachers Training College to train primary school teachers. The Zambia College of Agriculture is situated in the east of Monze township. The college trains not only the local farmers, but also the government officials of the Ministry of Agriculture. It has several experimental agricultural stations which breed new varieties of maize. This institution attracts students from other parts of Africa also. Its teaching staff is comprised of Zambians and others recruited from Britain and Asia.

After the Second World War, many Indian businessmen began to open shops at Monze. The Patel wholesale shop was the largest in the area. It supplied retail European and local goods to small African shop-keepers. The Patel family gradually became involved in many welfare activities in the district. They were instrumental in opening a Hindu Temple, which became the cultural center of the Indian community. They helped in building the Tagore Primary School, named after the great Indian poet Rabindranath Tagore. It became a noted school in the area and the large number of expatriates at Monze sent their children to the school. Its teaching staff were mostly Africans. In the 1960s, the Zambian Ministry of Education established the Monze Secondary School. Its first headmaster, W. Nyirenda, a cultured gentleman, later became the Education Minister of the Republic of Zambia. He was also a member of the Central Committee of President Kaunda's UNIP party.

Migration had been a boon and a curse to the people. Since agriculture was not well developed during the colonial period, the surplus young population from the farmers' families in Monze moved to mining cities on the southern side of the Zambezi River or to the copperbelt in the north of Zambia. Agriculture was thus neglected because most of the able-bodied men left for the wage-earning jobs elsewhere. Of course, the migrant laborers could send cash to the families back home. As the Africans neglected agriculture and the old farmer showed no great enterprise, the white farmers from Southern Rhodesia moved to the area. The white farmers had seen the benefits to be derived from the fertile soil in Southern Rhodesia. Now they became commercial farmers in Monze and Mazabuka areas which had adequate rainfall. The areas were good particularly for maize. Enterprising farmers such as Atkins and Paulson came to organize large farms, mostly near the rail line. The two British banks, namely Barclays and Standard, provided cash to farmers coming from Southern Rhodesia. Loans to African farmers were rare as they could not offer any guarantee. As a result most Africans remained essentially subsistence farmers. Wealth was concentrated in the hands of the immigrants whose entrepreneurship was noteworthy. No one would deny the contribution of Mr. Atkins and his family to the growth of the local economy. African peasants in Chief Monze's area were able to develop commercial agriculture despite some political and other obstacles. A small but important peasantry emerged by the middle of the present century. In fact, Monze and Mazabuka are two districts at present supplying food to many parts of Zambia. The indigenous commercial farmers contributed to the growth of Monze's economy.

It is relevant to make some observations on the political activities in the district. Harry Nkumbula, a school teacher and a resident of Namwala, a town not far from Monze, was the first significant politician to raise hopes for independence. He opposed the British creation of the Central African Federation based on the dominance of the White settlers of Southern Rhodesia. Paul Mambo of Lochinvar and Mainza Chona of Nampeyo came to organize local opposition to the Central African Federation, which had its headquarters in Salisbury. With the rise of astute politicians, such as Simon Kapwepwe and Kenneth Kaunda, both being Bemba-speaking national leaders, the Tonga-speaking leader Harry Nkumbula lost the support of the people of Zambia. But in the Southern Province Nkumbula had a strong base. The Monze district remained the stronghold of anti-Kaunda sentiment mainly because of the existence of the separate tribal spirit in the South. In

October, 1959, Mainza Chona of Nampeyo, Monze, left the African National Congress (ANC) and joined the United National Independence Party (UNIP) of Kaunda. The chiefs in the district were mostly passive in national politics.

Geographically, Monze has been well placed because it is in the maize belt and enjoys adequate rainfall. The climate is good for the sustained population growth. Politically, the district has earned a distinct place because many of its residents have become national politicians. Monze is an important railway station between Livingstone and Lusaka.

Basic Information Regarding Monze District[12]

Total area:	435,676 ha
Number of cattle in 1978:	200,000
Average arable area per person:	1.32 ha.
Average non-arable area per person:	4.35 acres.
Commercial farming area:	72,928 acres.
Grazing area per cattle:	1.9 ha.

Endnotes

1 Irving Kaplan, ed., *Zambia: A Country Study* (Washington, D.C.: The American University, 1979), pp. 80–83.

2 Ibid.

3 A.J. Wills, *An Introduction to the History of Central Africa* (London: Oxford University Press, 1985).

4 Irving Kaplan, ed., *Area Hand Book for Zambia* (Washington, D.C.: The Government Printing Office, 1968), pp. 80–81.

5 W.V. Brelsford, *The Tribes of Northern Rhodesia*, 1956.

6 Father Dominic Nchete of Mazabuka offered this explanation. Father Dominic Nchete, *History of Monze Chief* (1975), typescript.

7 Interviews with Chief Chona, July 5, 1978 at Nampeyo.

8 There is no written source about Fort Monze. I collected the information from elderly people who served in the security forces. Of course there is some factual information available from the District boma.

9 Information from the archives at Chikuni Mission.

10 Files at Monze Boma.

11 Interview with Fr. Flannery of Monze Secondary School.

12 Files at Monze Boma.

Chapter III

HISTORY OF CHIEFS IN MONZE DISTRICT

Before independence in 1964, there were six chiefs in the district. Their reputation and areas of chieftaincy varied. These chiefs' areas were (in sq. km.):[1]

1. Chief Monze   = 615.99
2. Chief Mwanza   = 536.21
3. Chief Chona   = 379.57
4. Chief Siamusonde   = 849.21
5. Chief Choongo   = 630.47
6. Chief Ufwenuka   = 200.70

There were 209 villages in Chief Monze; 54 in Chief Chona; 95 in Chief Choongo; 80 in Chief Mwanza; 56 in Chief Ufwenuka; 66 in Chief Siamusonde. Chief Siamusonde had the largest cattle population with 46,688, while Chief Chona had the lowest number of cattle with 10,266 in 1978. In a district with a human population of about 110,000 in 1978, the total number of cattle of 194,600 was quite high. Bulls, cows, and oxen were good assets to the people. These animals were the people's main investment. People in the rural areas had hardly any contact with the banks at Monze.

The names of the traditional councilors were as follows:[2]

CHIEF	RESIDENCES	COUNCILORS (1977)
Chief Monze	Mayanda /Katimba	Hachikonga Chikwala Simweete Mulangu
Chief Chona	Nampeyo	Dominic Mazuba Taule Mukonde Enock Hamutate and Samende

		Samende Mwanayanga
Chief Mwanza	Njola	Choombwa
		Chikani
		Hamalyangombe
Chief Siamusonde	Bweengwa	Chibwanta
		Lutumbo
		Hambwambwa
		Mwankanipe
		Chilomo
Chief Choongo	Nteme	Chikuni Hamwindu
		Moonga and Maimbo
Chief Ufwenuka	Chikuni	Abraham Mwiika Nzala
		Sikawala
		Hambale
		Munene Jophet
		Cheelo
		Chikonga

Some observations can be made regarding tribal names, chiefs' residences, and occupations of the councilors. First, the names were not European. The majority of the councilors said that they were not christians and were satisfied with the tribal religious customs and practices. Second, virtually all of them were selected by their people. Though a Western style election did not take place, they were chosen by popular consensus. Third, as regards the survival of these councilors, I found that many of them relied on purely subsistence farming. As Councilors, they helped their chiefs in deciding what communal celebrations could be organized, what new regulations could be introduced to make equitable use of lands, and what punishment could be given to defying members of the villages. In the absence of strict and rigorous modern government machinery, the councilors, supported by popular consensus, maintained political cohesion. This tribal tranquility was not disturbed with the setting up of regional and local government councils.

Chief Monze had his headquarters at Mayaba/Katimba; Chief Siamusonde at Bweengwa; Chief Choongo at Nteme; Chief Ufwenuka at Chikuni; Chief Chona at Nampeyo; Chief Mwanza at Njola. The number of chiefs' councilors varied from year to year. In 1975, the numbers of councilors were as follows: Chona had four; Choongo had four; Monze had four; Mwanza had three; Siamusonde had five; Ufwenuka had five. In 1978 the total number was 23 in all six areas. There were no Paramount Chiefs or Senior Chiefs in the district.

The size of the area of any particular chief did not signify his high or low position both in his society or outside. A chief could not expand his boundary because the people of another chief's area would not like to come under him unless forced to do so for various reasons. People under a particular chief belonged to a certain group with which they liked to be associated always. The chief and his people formed one group, like an extended family. There was a structural hierarchy; a chief was respected because he was a chief and yet it is equally true to suggest that his position was superior because he worked for his people.

Chief Monze

Chief Monze enjoyed most respect from the people throughout the district. Local traditions suggest that there had been always a chief for the Monze area. It is believed that the first chief was Mayaba. After his disappearance came Mutonga who appeared to be an ancestor of subsequent chiefs at Monze. Dr. David Livingstone came to the area and left a recorded impression which suggests that the influence of the chief at Monze went back two hundred years prior to 1855.

Some family records testify that Chief Haamiyanda Nchete ruled over ninety years during the nineteenth century. According to a tradition, when small-pox broke out in the area, the chief went to Chisekesi hill, about ten miles from Monze township, where he dug out some stones. He soaked these in a pot filled with water mixed with local medicine and gave this water to his people. This cured the infected people. Haamiyanda Nchete was the one whom the colonial administration contacted at an early stage of the coming of the British. A written note definitely suggests that he was locked up by the British at Kalomo in the first decade of the nineteenth century.

This recorded version regarding the imprisonment of the Monze Chief is corroborated by other sources. It appears that Monze Nchete sent an envoy to Zimbabwe in 1897 to contact Cecil Rhodes of the BSA Company. Rhodes told the envoy Liso Nzala that he was not the real authority to decide on the status of the territory. Rhodes told him that he could do nothing, but at the same time he was not happy that the envoy should go to England for political negotiations. In any case, Monze Nchete made preparations to go to England and collected money from the people of Monze for the journey overseas. Annoyed, the BSA Company ordered the arrest of the ambitious ruler of Monze. He was thus detained at the Kalomo jail in 1902. When the four Tonga boys, who had gone along with Father Moreau to Rhodesia, returned to the north of the Zambezi River, they were shocked at the news of chief's arrest. Father Moreau was disappointed to see that the chief, who had encouraged the missionaries to stay at Monze, had been arrested by the British agents. He and the four Tonga boys wished to meet with the arrested chief but the authorities refused. In 1906, Monze Nchete was released from the jail and was sent to his own area. He died in his own village in 1915. Monze Nchete was friendly with the Chikuni Mission, although he showed no keen desire to accept

Christianity. In fact, the acceptance of Christianity by any chief remained unclear. It appears that early chiefs in Monze did not accept Christianity. The Monze Chief I met in 1978 was nominally Christian in the sense that he attended Sunday church along with other Christians but in many respects he adhered to African ancestral worship.

Monze Nchete's successor was Chief Haamajani. He died in 1922 after a short rule and the chieftainship remained vacant for a year. The next chief was Longwani Mweemba, installed by the British. The colonial administration wanted several chiefs for the district in order to soften the local hostile attitude of the people toward the foreign rule. In 1924, Chief Monze accompanied the District Commissioner (DC) to go around in search of some new chiefs. Chief Monze explained to the people that things had changed and the people should accept the reality of the arrival of the alien administration.

Upon selection, the new chief was given by the colonial officers the official documents, a clerk, and a walking stick. For a long time these chiefs were called "box chiefs" because they were created by the British, who gave them boxes containing documents. This was a derogatory term. These newly created chiefs were told by the Commissioner that they were independent of the Chief Monze and should rule according to the local traditions subject to certain conditions. Gradually they became spokesmen for the British in their respective areas. But outside the Southern Province, people still knew only Chief Monze. The migrant workers going to work in Southern Rhodesia and South Africa used to write, in their legal documents, to have come from Chief Monze area.

The British administration exerted some political influence over Monze. Longwani Mweemba was the cousin of Haamajani. Mweemba was sick and weak, but the British reached a compromise to the effect that so long as Mweemba was alive no one else would be regarded as chief. Before the death of Mweemba in 1960, Rice Hamalambo Mongonti was permitted by the British to act as temporary chief from 1954. Mongonti was deposed in 1964 just before independence because he sided with the nationalists. Mongonti was even locked up for two years. Penn, the District Commissioner of Mazabuka, called a meeting to announce the deposition of Mongonti, and asked the people to select their own chief. A meeting was held under the presidency of Chief Chona who was then the chief executive of the Plateau Tonga Native Authority. The meeting failed to elect a chief.

On December 15, 1959, Penn, the District Commissioner, called another meeting at Patel's Store, a wholesale shop run by an Indian family. Only headmen were allowed to attend. In defence of the deposition of Mongonti, the British officer told the assembled headmen,

> I want to make it clear that Mongonti was deposed simply because he has been incapable of administering the area. The other point of activity – supporting the African National Congress matter – is a very small one, though, of course, the chief being a government representative must not belong to any political organization. The decision taken by the government is final.

As to the election of the next chief, the District Commissioner supported that someone closely related to the aged chief, should be selected as the new chief. One candidate was Cletus Kapapa. The headman Luayaba presided.[3]

After the election was held according to the local rules, the DC announced, "Cletus Kapapa has been elected beating three other candidates. I have consulted the members of the Tonga Native Authority, namely Chiefs Chona, Siamusonde, Ufwenuka, Mwanachingwala. They agree to Cletus's selection as suitable candidate." After this pronouncement, another candidate Rice

Haamalambo argued that he was still strong enough to rule and that Cletus should take over after his death. Cletus was confirmed by the British administration.[4]

From this narrative, partly based on oral traditions and partly on records at the Monze Boma, several significant points emerge. First, nationalism had already touched the local chiefs, and the DC was opposed to the chief because he was aligned with the African National Congress, then agitating against the Central African Federation. During the election the DC declared that the Monze Chief was deposed due to his inefficiency. But there were no charges or complaints against the chief. The chief's association with the Congress was a disqualification. The motive of the DC was made clear when he put forward the idea of partition of Monze chieftainship. He remarked, "This area is too big for one court. The government is thinking of dividing this into two." Soon under pressure, the DC was forced to declare, "There is no rushing into the matter." Second, the colonial authority was very much involved in the selection of even the chieftainship in Monze which usually carried high respect among the people. Third, the colonial administration attached great significance to the Monze Chief. Incidentally, this confirms the local belief that Chief Monze had always been special and powerful.

Chief Choongo

Many elders in Choongo's area inherited a story suggesting that the ruling clan arrived from Southern Rhodesia in the early part of the nineteenth century. The general public believe the story. Chief Choongo's court kept some documents dealing with the history of early chiefs.

The family traditions, as preserved by the elders as well as the chief, offer some details about the chiefs' background. There was an inter-tribal war in Southern Rhodesia in 1818 when tribes migrated to the north. A group of related people crossed the Zambezi River by swimming north. This group was led by a woman named Nzala. The whole group came to be known as Beetwa. At that time there was no other clan by that name. They did not settle on the shores of the Zambezi. Three persons called Zulanika Munekopa, Tweseka Mweemba, and Mangezi Mweemba left the banks of the Zambezi for the interior. They stopped at a place called Singooch. At night, Zulanika was killed by a lion. The place where the lion attacked the group was not far from the present-day agricultural farm of Paulson Mweenga of Monze township.

The leadership of the group was then taken by Tweseka Mweemba who buried the dead body of Zulanika. Upon getting the message of the death of their relative, fourteen more persons arrived from Southern Rhodesia to mourn the death. Thereafter Mbala Mumbwe married Tweseka. He established himself as Tweseka's advisor and later on shared power with his wife. One Choongo, Mwanampongwe, was jealous of this love between Tweseke and Mbala and so killed Mbala and declared himself as Chief Choongo to rule an area not far from the present-day Monze. The British did not see him. It was Chief Choongo Hamanchenga, the second chief, who came in contact with the British administration. Hamanchenga was a half brother of Mwanampongwe. When Hamanchenga died, Munakembe, the younger brother of Mwanampongwe, succeeded him. The fourth chief was Benjamin Bbandika, nephew of the first chief.

Records kept at the Nteme Court indicate that Benjamin Bandika claimed the chieftaincy when another man from Namwala could not be the chief. In an application to the DC at Mazabuka dated June 5, 1932, Benjamin Bandika wrote:

> When the old Choongo died, I, Benjamin Bandika, was then a little
> boy. Therefore the man placed Hamachenga, in the place of Choongo

as a chief. He was only a Counsellor. Again when Hamachenga had died, Munakembe succeded him by the order of the people, and after that there came Kazoka, from Namwala District. He took away the badge of chieftainship from Munakembe, and placed it on Hangaila. He then brought him to Mazabuka to show him how to be the chief of Banakaila, and he was accepted... That Munakembe was a brother of Choongo and was the right heir or successor, although they rejected him as a chief of Bankaila. It seems to me, Benjamin, that they were all usurpers. They do not understand what government says. Government says that all people are free from slavery. Now this is my question, that why some people are still robbing the things of others. When I see the section of Banakaila, I found out, that the people are still in slavery. Therefore, I want the government to understand that old Chief Choongo, they were five brothers, and one sister. These were the owners of the country of Banakaila.

Then, I, Benjamin, was born to the sister of the old Chief Choongo. The Chief Choongo then was my real uncle. Now all the unsettled cases, which my uncle old Choongo left, they are imputed to me. I am in the responsibility to pay them...

I still have one important question to ask. How Kazoka, a man from Namwala District, been able to come in the section of mine and elect a man to be the Chief of Banakaila. This is my question which I place before the Government of Mazabuka.

Hangaila quarrelled with Benjamin Bandika and was forced to surrender the throne to him. A claimant to the throne said that Bandika was a far off man from Beetwas clan as his mother belonged to the Baunga Clan and his father to the Munsaka clan. Benjamin received school education and was clever. He went to negotiate with the whites, some of whom were solicitors. He extended his campaign by going to the then Barotseland to bribe Paramount Chief Lewanika, who had some influence over Tongaland at that time.

After the death of Benjamin, Shellen Hanagila claimed to be the rightful owner of the chieftainship. He said, "It was me, Sheleen

Hangaila, who first received the colonial court-box for his this court." But it was Amos Tela who actually succeded Benjamin Bandika Choongo on July 27, 1971 as Chief Choongo. Benjamin was the uncle of Amos Tela.

A description of Chief Choongo's election in 1971 gives an idea of the system adopted in electing a chief in Monze district. At the time of the election, there was an assembly of all the chiefs in the district and some villagers. Chiefs Siamusonde, Mwanza, Ufwenuka, and Monze were present. Seventy-nine headmen from Choongo's area and 188 tribal elders and relatives representing two clans that claimed the right to succession also gathered. About 250 villagers were also present to witness the succession procedure.

In accordance with traditional practices, the chiefs jointly presided over the deliberations. Their spokeman was Chief Ufwenuka. He said:

> We have come as chiefs to help in finding out in which line you are going to choose a chief. We are merely observers who have come not to impose a decision or to make orders but to witness your selection of a successor to the late Chief Choongo. We urge you to choose only one chief as there is only one throne. In the first instance, we are going to seek the opinion of the relatives or clansmen of the deceased chief who have claimed right to the succession about the person whom they have chosen; we will then after disagreement among relatives, ask the opinion of the headmen.

At one corner were seated a group of relatives of the deceased Chief Choongo of the Unga clan and at another were a group of the Beetwa clan. Chief Siamusonde asked whether the people had agreed on a candidate. Amos Tela rose from the Choongo clan and all in the clan agreed that he had been chosen by them as their chief. There were three candidates from the Beetwa clan: Ngawmu, Paul Chiloba and Mulebwente. Ngawmu was neither proposed or seconded. He was considered eliminated from the contest. Chief Monze then asked which one of the remaining two the clan preferred for chief. Chiloba had been nominated by only one person and therefore could not be regarded as a candidate for the Beetwa. Chief Ufwenuka then rose and said:

> It seems that we have reached a point of conflict and as such an election was inevitable and should be conducted. But first we would like to know who of you have objected to the other person's standing?

Sheleni Hangala said that Chilabo had a better claim to stand because he was a full Mweetwa who was in the line of succession. Hangaila explained the family tree as follows:

> Mukanamwela was the first women chief and upon her death was succedded by Namoza. Hamunkoyo was after him. Hamanchenga succeded, and after him was Sheleni Hangaila, a Mweetwa.

He said during this time, the throne went to Benjamin Bandika, the late Chief Choongo, of the Munga clan. Mayanda rose up to state a case for his candidate Mulebwente. He said that the chieftainship should go back to the Beetwa clan because to do so was not to allow the chieftainship to drift to the Unga clan. Mulebwente remarked that he did not see any reason why the Beetwa people should try to isolate themselves and separate. He said that they were not related to the Choongo clan and that was the reason why the throne should not be given to the late Chief Choongo by Europeans at the headquaters of Chief Monze. He added that he was not in line of succession. Hangaila said that the late Chief Choongo was made chief at a tribal council held at chief Monze's headquarters and was subsequently confirmed as chief by the government.

The Chief Monze then asked the group of Baba Choongo to state their case. Timothy Mwanapingwe asked the question, "If a person works and keeps money when that person dies to whom does he give that money?" All the people replied, "To the clan." He continued that Choongo Mwanapongwe was the first chief in Chief Choongo's area. After his death, his third brother became chief. As he was an old man, he appointed Hangaila, a Mweetwa, as Regent because his nephew, Benjamin Bandika, the heir to the throne was at school. In 1933, Benjamin Bandika came out from school and claimed his chieftainship. At a tribal council held at Chief Choongo's headquarters, Benjamin Bandika was installed as Chief Choongo.

The chiefs discussed the method of election, and in the event that the people wanted an election, a grain of maize was to be distributed to each voter and voters would drop the grain in either of the plates of the candidates. A District Messenger was secretly sent to bring a maize cob and two plates which were concealed from the people. The candidates were then called to the stand in front of the village headmen and relatives of the candidates. Amos Tela and Nyalati Mulebwente stood in front of the recording table. All village headmen were asked to raise their hands so that they could be separated from the people who had assembled. They were seventy-nine in all. All people said that there was no person in the file who was not related to them. The same procedure applied to the members of the Beetwa clan who were fifty-eight in all. Two small yellowish plates were placed in front of the two election agents. The one near the filing voters marked Beetwa and the other far off was marked Unga to denote the clans of the candidates. The District Secretary saw that there was no lobbying as voting was taking place.

Village headmen filed in. As each of them entered, he was given a grain of maize. The grains of maize were counted first by the Chiefs and were then recounted by the election agents. Headmen in favor of the Unga clan were forty-four and headmen in favor of the Beetwa clan were thiry-five. The figures were added up and balanced with the seventy-nine that had been recorded outside the election room. The relatives then filed in and each one was given a grain of maize as he entered. Relatives voted according to their clans. When the voting ended, the election agents and the returning officers noted the sixty Unga clans men and women cast their votes. An election agent for Unga who did not cast his vote was given one grain of maize to vote. The figure for the Unga rose to sixty-one, the same figure that had been counted outside before voting took place. For the Beetwa clan, at first, fifty-six voted for their clan but after enquiring outside, an elderly man was found not to have voted. He was brought in to vote and the number rose to fifty-seven in favor of the Beetwa clan. One Mweetwa clansman apparently made up his mind and did not turn up to vote. Amos Tela had forty-four village headmen and sixty-one traditionalists casting for him, bringing the total votes he polled to 105. Nyeleti Mulebwente had thirty-five village headmen and fifty-seven traditionalists voting for him bringing the total votes he polled to ninty-two. Amos Tela was therefore elected Chief Choongo to succeed his late uncle. He was brought in front of all the people who were cheering with joy. The succession of the chieftainship is neither matrineal or partineal. That is why there is an election whenever a chief is to be chosen.

Family Tree of Chief Choongo:
1. The first Chief Choongo was Choongo Mwanampongwe.
2. The second was Hamanchenga, half brother of the first.
3. The third was Munakembe, youngest brother of the first chief.
4. The fourth chief was the Benjamin Bandika, nephew of the first.

5. Benjamin had four sisters whose male children were eligible
    for succession.

It appears that the colonial authorities were very much interested
in maintaining links with the ruling Choongo Chief. On several
occasions the chiefs wrote the DC at Mazabuka.[5]

Chief Mwanza

The history of the Mwanza chiefdom has been reconstructed
mainly from interviews with the chief and his councilors in August,
1978. According to the chief, the dominant clan – the Baleya – came
from the area near the northern bank of the Zambezi River. The
clan first settled in an area known as Matawaazyanza in Monze
district. From there they moved to Njola.

Chief Japhet Chidamba, whom I met in 1978, came to the
traditional throne in 1939. According to the popular estimate he
was the longest serving chief in the district. He took over as chief
from his grand uncle Sing'anga Chidamba. The system of
succession was matrilineal. A grand son of Chigaboga, he had five
wives at that time. Two of his seven wives had died. I was
introduced to the head wife and tried to get some information
through my interpreter Bruno Mwiinga, regarding the actual
mechanism of family relationships. It was not as simple as it would
appear to Westerners. First, the head wife was not simply another
wife. She allocated cash obtained from sales of agricultural produce
and livestock and bought necessities for the families. These
included kerosene oil and tools. It appears that she had the decisive
voice in the budget. Second, she maintained very harmonious
relations with all other wives. Jealousy was virtually absent. Third,
the chief treated the wives affectionately. Last, all felt that there
was nothing wrong in marrying several women. It helped
procreation, a vital need in the face of high mortality rate for

children. Also, wives helped in the field work. According to the local social ethos, wives were helping hands.

I talked to three traditional councilors, Choombwa, Chikuni, and Hamalyangombe, to get an idea about the political aspects of the chief's rule. Before Japhet Chidamba came to the throne there was an election held to decide between the chief and his uncle Gideon Mujampa who was not very popular. The actual system was different from the Western election process. There was no counting of votes, no ballot of any sort. It was the consensus arrived at amicably. The consensus, according to the local calculations, removed suspicion and also showed no victor or vanquished. After all, the tribal ethos suggests that any friction is dangerous in the hostile natural environment. Man has no control over his surroundings, and as such friendship is the ultimate resort.

Chief Mwanza was the leader of the area called Njola Mafuwa, a place which was supposed to be a burial ground for war victims. These wars were fought between the Lozi, Ndebele, and the Tonga. The first tribal leader was a woman. When the Europeans came to the area, they found that the people in the area respected her highly, and thus regarded her as chief. She was respected because she had herbs which people applied to avoid being conquered by enemies. The locals used to go to her to pray for rain. By clapping and praying to the spirits, this women could bring rain.

The following is a list of chiefs who were in the throne at Njola:
1. Chieftainsee Zabunda.
2. Chibumbu (Chief Mwanza), the son of Zabunda.
3. Sing'anga, a nephew of Chibumbu.
4. Japhet Chidamba, a grand-nephew of Sing'anga.

There were two sacred places – Malende and Nyambe. Twice a year, the people led by the chief used to go to the area to offer sacrifices. Traditional beer known as Lwiindi used to be offered to ancestral spirits to placate them. This celebration generally took

place in December. Communal beer drinking and dancing were
important features. Another celebration was observed in October
during the dry season. After the communal prayer the people
burned a black goat and ate its meat without salt.[6]

Chief Siamusonde

It is believed that when Dr. Livingstone came to Monze district,
he asked Chief Monze whether there was a chief in the west of
Monze. Chief Monze replied that there was a powerful person
known as Namusonde. Dr. Livingstone then met and decorated him
as Chief Siamusonde. This is reported to have taken place in 1858.
Oral tradition suggests that Siamusonde had the physical energy
to fight. It is said that the chief alone could fight one hundred
enemies and kill them all. He is believed to have had the brains to
arrange a fight. He used to settle disputes in the Bweengwa area
of Monze district. Chief Monze admired him for those reasons. He
often consulted with Chief Siamusonde about war and other
matters of common interest. These were wars between the Lozi and
the Tonga and also the Matabele of Rhodesia.

A paper kept in the chief's court has the following list of chief's
names:

1. Malambo Hamusonde (1862–1920)
2. Hanambe Mulube (1920–1923)
3. Kulumbwe Himalumba (1923–1947)
4. Simuyobe Ntambo (1947–1950)
5. Munakambwe Mulungu (1950–1953)
6. Miyoba Hamusonde (1953–)

Malambo Hamusonde was succedded by his younger brother,
Hanambe Mulube. Mulube was succedded by his nephew
Kulumbwe Himalumbe and later by Simuyobe Ntambo. Simuyobe
Ntambo was not in any way united by ties to consanguinity with
Himalumba. It is believed that when Himalumba died, most of his

relatives were also dead and others were too young to take over.

Hunankambwe who took over in 1950 was a son of Chinyama Malambo Hamusonde, the first Chief. Miyoba Hamusonde, a step brother of Chinyama Malambo Hamusonde, and therefore uncle of Munankambwe. He therefore took over the chieftainship from his nephew. The system of succession is either patrilineal or matrileneal. If there is any nephew still living, he would succed as Chief Siamusonde because the system of succession shows a marked matrilineal inclination.

Chief Ufwenuka

According to popular traditions prevalent in the area, the first chief was recognized because he had leadership quality. He was particularly good in dispute settlements. Ufwenuka Shimweemba was the first chief. He lived a long life. He welcomed the Catholic missionaries because he wanted to set up a school with the help of the missionaries. Missionaries were eager to establish schools to spread the English language, a key to reading the Bible.

The second chief was Haachilima Ufwenuka, the uncle of Chief Shimweeba. People in the area affirmed that he had a brief chieftaincy because he died of flu. The third chief was Chisvuo. He was made a temporary chief by Ufwenuka Shimweeba because sons of the previous chief were too young. The temporary chief was told that he would be replaced when the sons would grow up. In any case, according to official records kept at the court, he ruled for sixteen years. The next chief was a women called Namweemba Ufwenuka, who was the daughter of the first Chief Shimweemba. She also ruled for sixteeen years. She was married to Jakalani Malila who was a cousin of Namweemba Ufwenuka. He jointly ruled the area till 1952. Shadreck Nyanga started to rule from September 1952. He took over from Namweema Ufwenuka. Nyanga had western education and introduced modern agriculture to the area. In this respect, he was aided by the Chikuni Mission. Besides maize, he introduced produce beans, ground nuts and vegetables.

The Chief Ufwenuka whom I met in 1978 was Shadreck Nyanga, who was born in 1928. He belonged to the Beetwa clan. His official residence was at Chikuni, which means a country. At times, he lived in Chipembere village, about six miles from the Chikuni government court. When the BSA Co. Officials arrived in Chikuni, they met with Chief Ufwenuka Shimweemba at his palace in Chikuni. He was already recognized by his people as chief.

The sucession procedure was without a pattern. An uncle took over from his nephew. At one time, the throne was given to a cousin, then to the daughter of the first chief, then to the brother of the first chief. What is clear is that the succession lineage was partly partineal. Elections used to be held in cases of succession of disputes. In fact, chiefs had no relationship to one another as it was the case in the Western and Northern provinces of Zambia. When a chief died, it became difficult to appoint a heir to the throne. It was not necessary that only sons would inherit.

Chief Chona

The first Chief Chona was not a "traditional" chief but a leader who rose to prominence because of his special qualities. During the early colonial period, the British chose to set up a "tribal" administration and gave recognition to several chiefs. Some newly created Tonga chiefs, other than Monze chiefs, were given a box containing official documents and two capsus. But the Chona Chief did not belong to these "Box Chiefs." The first known chief, Beenzu Chona, came to be recognized on his own right. He had enemies, who were all around. The Lozi invaders were after valuable skins, the Ndebele were looking for women and cattle. "Life was short and brutish." Beenzu used to resort to spiritual deeds to ward off incoming enemies. Immediately after he saw enemies coming to his headquaters, he used to go to his mystic abode and cause a very cold wind to blow. The enemies, instead of fighting, burned the handles of their spears and made fire to keep themselves warm. The people were saved. Thus the mystic leader turned to be an earthly ruler in the Chona area.

Beenzu Chona belonged to the Bakonke clan. According to family tradition, it came from the Demo at Nudimunene which is now in Chief Siamasonde's area. Beenzu Chona came to settle in what is now called the Monze district. He found the Baleya clans of Sichangu there. Beenzu married a girl from that clan. He was clever and intelligent. According to tradition, he was an African healer able to cure almost all types of diseases. People from neighboring villages came to him for treatment.

Beenzu's palace was called Nampeyo, which means coldness. Whenever the Bulozi came to the area, they used to call at his Palace. He gave them beasts to eat. The Bulozi asked him to collect his skins from all over the area including Gwembe valley. They frequented his Palace to collect skins as taxes. As they left the area, he gave them young beautiful girls to carry the collected skins. Before the arrival of the Europeans, Beenzu was thus recognized as Chief of Nampeyo.

Local traditions suggest that the people of the Baleya clan asked him to own the area as he had done so much for the protection and care of his people. The Lozi invaders could do little harm as he was tactful and clever. Beenzu thus remained the natural chief of the Chona area. After Beenzu's death, Nankambula, the nephew of Beenzu Choona, became the Chief. He ruled for a short time only. People feared that the clan might collapse if chiefs lived as short as Nankambula lived.

It was widely believed by the Chona elders and family members that the niece of the Chona Nangoma Malembwe, who was the great-grandmother of present Chief Simon Moomba, was entered with spirits of rain-making. She asked the people to construct small houses at the graves of the late Mahwali and Chona's grave. These are still considered sacred. Whenever the traditional beer, Lwiindi, is made, it is taken there. There are small huts near the grave side. Skins from black cows or black goats are used as fibers for the construction and maintenance of these huts.

There is a strong belief that the next chief Haamatu, nephew of Nakambula Chona, was a slave. To celebrate the accession of Haamatu, a lot of beer was brewed. Before beer was served, Brake Nachimwenda became annoyed and broke most of the beer containers. A woman named Nangoma lied to save her son from the rampaging Nachimwenda. When Haamatu saw the mad activities of Nachmwenda, Haamatu fled from the village. He fled Nampeyo for Namaila, an area now under Chief Haanjalika. While fleeing away he took with him a sacred ox tail which is traditionally kept by the chiefs. When he reached Namaila, he became rain-maker because of the ox tail he stole. When Namukamba, a member of the Chona clan, heard this, he searched for and found Nachimwenda. He brought back the special tail. All the members of the Chona clan, who had fled Nampeyo with Haamatu, were brought back by Namukamba Chona, who by then took over the chieftainship.

He ruled up to 1927. Meanwhile, a confusion was created in the chieftainship. Family traditions suggest that there was a break in the succession. When the British Provinical Administrators visited the area, they were misinformed that Chief Mwanza was in actual control of the Chona area. For about three years, Chief Mwanza was the de facto ruler. It was Namukamba who brought back the glory of Beenzu Chona. He laid strong claims on the chieftainship. After all, the Chonas were the saviours in times of Lozi incursions.

The Tonga used to send precious skins of animals to Lewanika periodically. So the taxation imposed by the British was also at first welcomed in general. The British used the taxes to build schools and hospitals. The people in the Chona area welcomed the development brought about by the Colonial Administration. Soon, Chief Chona along with other neighboring chiefs, became agents of the government. His traditional authority began to disappear. Also, missionaries began to spread new values to counteract the traditional beliefs.

There are some clear pictures about the history of one Chief Haameja Chona (1927–1951). He was hard working and educated. Haameja Chona attended a Local Government school at Chalimbana near Lusaka in 1949. He attracted many people to Nampeyo from Chief Mwanza's area in 1931. He did not neglect his traditional duties. With his encouragement, new primary schools were set up and new mission stations were established in remote areas.

Haameja had two sons, Mainza Mathias Chona and Mark Chona. Though not so well "educated" himself, Haameja saw to it that all his children went to school, attended and did not drop out, because he wanted his children to have "wisdom." This he possessed himself to a high degree. Although Haameja was a 'minor' chief, his great sense of justice attracted many people to take their appeal cases to him. A courageous man, Haameja died in April, 1951, while trying to save others cattle from a lion. He was also survived by three daughters.[7]

Mainza Chona, born in January, 1930, at Nampeyo near Monze was educated at Chona Out School, Chikuni Catholic Mission School, and Munali Government Secondary School. As a clerk-interpreter at the High Court in Livingstone, from 1951 to 1955, young Chona impressed people with his efficiency and a sense of discipline. At this time, he composed a novel in Chitonga language, and the book was published in 1952 as *Kabuca Uleta Tunji*, which won the Margaret Wong Medal in 1956. He earned a scholarship in 1955 from the government to study law at Gray's Inn in London.

Although he became a barrister, he was unable to get a job upon his return, and so he became a typist. Then, frustrated, Chona turned to politics which suited him. Mainza Chona has a pleasant character.

Since the Zambia African National Congress was banned, Chona joined the African National Congress, hoping to make it more progressive. He tried to persuade Kenneth Kaunda to challenge Harry Nkumbula for the party leadership because most of the educated youths of Northern Rhodesia did not like Nkumbula's conservative approach to political advancement. Within the ANC, Chona challenged Nkumbula himself. In 1959, Chona was elected president of one faction of the ANC. His speeches on national issues began to attract a large following, and he was quickly welcomed into the United National Independence Party (UNIP) which was becoming the most popular in Zambia. He was president of the UNIP until Kenneth Kaunda was released from detention. In 1960 Kaunda became President of the party and Mainza Chona became Vice President.

Chona visited several countries to maintain contacts with political developments in Africa. He stayed outside Zambia for some time because the Lusaka government brought a charge of sedition against him. Intellectually, he became so involved in party politics and soon became the editor of the party paper, *The Voice of UNIP*.

From 1961 to 1962, he was the Secretary of UNIP and after independence in 1964 he became a Member of Parliament. From 1964 to 1966 he was the Minister of Justice. From 1968 to 1969 he was the Minister for Central Province. He also worked as Zambia's Ambassador to the United States. In 1970 he became Vice President of the Republic of Zambia and thus became the second most important person after President Kaunda. In August, 1973, he became Zambia's Prime Minister under the new constitution. Internally his most important task was to head the commission on the new constitution. The Chona Commission which he headed made many of the recommendations, which were ultimately implemented in the new constitution. In 1975 he resigned as Prime Minister due to ill health.

Mainza Chona's brother Mark Chuunyu Chona was born in June, 1934, at Nampeyo. He was educated at Chona Elementary School from 1943 to 1948, Chikuni School from 1948 to 1954, and Munali Secondary School from 1954 to 1958. His education was truly international. He obtained his B.A. degree in History and Economics at Salisbury University. He also studied at Cambridge University and in both Canada and the U.S. in the 1960s.

He served the Zambian government in various capacities. He was appointed District Officer in June 1963 in the Eastern Province and was posted at Katete. He was then appointed to the staff of Kenneth Kaunda a month before independence in October, 1964. He also worked as Senior Principal Secretary responsible for provincial affairs. After marriage in December, 1964, he left the Presidential Office to become the Permanent Secretary at the Ministry of Foreign Affairs, a post he held for three years. In 1968 he became the Presidents international representative and was sent to several countries as a trouble-shooter. He had little interest in domestic politics. President Kaunda relied on him as keen a negotiator.

Simon Mumba was installed as Chief on October 5, 1951, succedding Haameja Chona. He had a rival party from his uncle, James Syalukala, who was then the Court Assessor at Nampeyo Court. Simon was at that time 30 years old. The colonial government gave him the official recognition as chief of Nampeyo Court on February 5, 1951. His father's name was Thadewa Makondo and his mother's name was Sikaya Cheepa.

In 1930, Simon went to school at Chikuni and stayed there to complete his Standard Seven. He then studied at the Elementary

Teachers' College at Mazabuka. He taught in Catholic schools from 1938 to 1942. He then worked as an agricultural assistant for five years. He went to Britain in April, 1961, to study Local Government and Public Administration at Oxford. While in Britain he was attached to Eton Rural District in Windsor Castle. On return he served the colonial administration in many respects. He worked in the African Representative Council, Provincial Council, District Education Authority, and Native Authority at Monze. Appointed by the District Commissioner, Sir Evelyn Hone, he worked as the Chairman of the Plateau Tonga Native Authority from 1956–1960. He was decorated with a certificate of Honor by Governor Evelyn Hone. After independence of Zambia he was elected to the House of Chiefs which became a part of the Zambian Legislature.

The Tonga society is matrilineal. Forming the direct line, the descendants from the mother are heirs to the property of the deceased. The successors to the chief and in some cases even to the village headmen must be descendants from the mother's side. But the system of succession among the Chonas is not rigid. In fact, cases of succession are dealt with as they come. The successor is chosen by his relatives, and when there is more than one candidate then an election is arranged. In the election process, there is an element of democracy.

The people of the Chona area follow a particular pattern in the elopement of girls. Anyone who elopes a girl should take or bring her back with one beast, such as an ox for mufwundundu but not two beasts as other tribes do. Afterwards three more beasts have to be paid to complete the case.

Though the modern administration of the government governs the area, minor political and economic disputes are still settled by the chief. Aided by traditional Councilors, Dominic Mazuba, Taule Mukonde, Enock Hamutete, Samende, and Mwanayanga, the chief commands considerable respect from all fifty-four villages of the Chief Chona area.

Traditionally, locally made beer is offered to ancestral spirits to placate them. Communal drinking and dancing are the main features of ceremonies. To welcome rains, prayers are held and the Chief leads his people. Communal prayers are also held during harvesting time. Sometimes a sheep or a goat is sacrificed to please the fore-fathers.

Royal Hunting. The annual royal hunting expedition takes place on top of a small sacred mountain called Chisoboyo. Common people are not normally allowed to hunt on the hill-top without the chief's consent. There is a hidden hoe in a hole in the mountain. During drought a member of Sakonka clan or one related to the chief is sent to check this hoe. When there is moisture on it that signifies that the rains are to be abundant that year. When there is no moisture that signifies that rains would be scarce in that year.

Usually a day is announced for the hunt. A bush is burnt. Three days later, the rain would come. When it is not done the rain would be scarce and it would be the chief's responsibility to see that a black cow, or a black goat is killed. This means that ancestral spirits forgave the mistake done by the chief and it would rain. If somebody else burns the bush accidentally, the ancestors would be annoyed. The person who burnt the bush accidentally is asked to contribute something, such as a goat, or a cow, which would be sacrificed. Before the hunt somebody goes to the mountain, gathers wild fruits, and takes them back home to make a special drink.

In spite of the spread of some new "isms," the tradition is still going on. Time has changed but beliefs are inherent and strong.[8]

Fig. 2: House of the Chonas

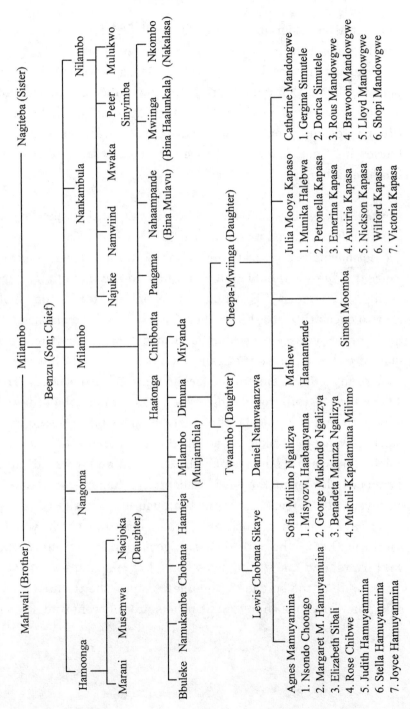

Endnotes

1 Files at Monze Boma; interviews.

2 Files at Monze Boma.

3 Based on interviews.

4 Files at Chief Chona.

5 Files at Chief Choongo.

6 Files at Chief Mwanza.

7 Files at Chief Chona.

8 Ibid.

Chapter IV

MISSIONARIES IN MONZE

Christianity was introduced into the southern region of Zambia in the late nineteenth century by several missionary societies inspired by Dr. David Livingstone, who died in 1873. The earliest missionary work was among the Bemba and Lozi. In trying to convert the important chiefs, the missionaries wished to gain influence among the general population. Despite efforts by the missionaries, there were only a few converts because the Western missionaries demanded complete renunciation of traditional beliefs. It was difficult for the local people to give up polygamy, bride wealth, ancestral worship, and witchcraft. However, it appears that missionaries were successful in remote areas where mission stations and outposts were established.

There are six dioceses including Monze. The Roman Catholics were initially more successful than their rivals. The Anglican Church had some success in the district also. Many of the successful farmers in the district were members of the Seventh-Day Adventist Church. However, the great majority of the interior farmers remained committed to traditional beliefs.

Chikuni Mission

The history of the Chikuni Mission is partly based on the Zambezi Mission Records (ZMR), notes on the Chikuni Mission preserved by Fr. Moreau, interviews with the priests at Chikuni, and some miscellaneous records kept at the Chikuni Mission.

Several attempts were made form Southern Rhodesia to set up a mission in Northern Rhodesia. In 1880, two Fathers and a Brother crossed the Zambezi River to arrive in the southern part of Northern Rhodesia, and attempted to set up a mission station. In 1889 more enquiries were made by Fr. Barthelemy. Through the good offices of Major Coryndon of the BSA Co., permission of the Paramount Chief of Barotseland was obtained. Cecil Rhodes also requested the Jesuit Fathers to come to Northern Rhodesia. He even offered material assistance.

It was decided in 1902 to go ahead with an expedition to the Zambezi. The Jesuit Fathers in Southern Rhodesia had always been interested in expansion. One motive was to defeat the work of the rival churches. The Monze Chief was well known and the area was climatically ideal for prolonged habitation of white settlers. Father Prestage of Empandeni in Southern Rhodesia made arrangements for a small but well organized expedition to the Tonga-land. He was accompanied by Fr. Moreau, a dedicated and determined man of action. Among other things, the expedition had a scotch-cart, 2 oxen, a horse and a donkey. It took the travellers 54 days to reach the Zambezi River near the southern border of Northern Rhodesia. After crossing the river, the party proceeded north to Kalomo, which was the center of the BSA Co. administration. Fr. Coryndon was the Administrator. He wished to establish political control at Monze. It was suspected that the old chief of Monze was creating disaffection among the Tongas. So the British officers wanted the missionaries to pacify the people and the chief.

The Jesuits had a strong desire to set up mission stations among the Batongas. Dr. David Livingstone had already met the chief who was interested in mission work. In a private letter written on July 20, 1902, Fr. Moreau wrote from Kalomo:

...for years I had an eye on Monze [Chief Monze]; he is fairly big chief, the biggest left without missionaries, and we could have all his country reserved to us as the P.M.S. [Paris Missinary Society] has taken Lewanika's [Barotseland]. Even in the event of choosing Karenga, as it is or will be on the railway, I think we must try by all means to secure Monze to the Catholic Church. I think we ought to occupy it at once, sending there boys from Chisawasha [in Southern Rhodesia], if we cannot go there ourselves.[1]

Other missionaries also reported about the area. For example, the Rev. Anderson of the Seventh Day Adventist Church stated, in his *On the Trail of Livingstone*:

> He [Chief BSA Co. Official at Kalomo] suggested that I go into the Monze District, about a hundred miles further to the north-east, and there open our mission work. The reason he wanted us to go there was that Old Monze, the Chief "rain-doctor" of the Batongas, had started a rebellion the year before, and they desired a missionary located in his district to keep watch over him. The late Mr. Cecil Rhodes once told me that he found missionaries to be much better for keeping the natives quiet than the soldiers, and certainly a good deal cheaper. So the administrators [of the BSA Co.] desired us to settle near the restive chief - and report any disorders that might occur in his district.

The Catholic farmers were impressed by the beautiful Batonga plateau. As one farmer said, "Certainly there could not have been more beautiful antelopes in Eden than those we saw all over the Batonga Plain."[2] On the northern side of Monze, the Catholic Fathers came across a large fig tree surrounded by a palisade making a perfect enclosure. In the center, they saw a grave of the old Chief Monze whom Dr. Livingstone had met. It was reported that the grave had hoes, beer pots, calabashes, and some grain inside. Chief Monze was the great rain-maker and the "wizard of the north." The graveyard was a kind of Tonga temple called "Malende," rendered sacred by the remains of a chief much respected in the area.

The two Jesuit Fathers came to know that Chief Monze had long been in contact with the whites. According to them, he was a progressive man with a shot gun and fly switch. He was five feet and nine inches tall, "of spare build, intelligent looking and active in his movements." He was about forty years old at that time, but according to Father Prestage, Monze's krall was a "perfect disgrace; no encloseurs, no order, while the huts had a most wretched appearence."

Despite pegging out of the Karenga Farm and the grant of twenty thousand acres from the chartered BSA Company, Monze (later called Chikuni Mission) was selected as the possible site for the Catholic Mission. Fr. Moreau wrote, "The latter [Karenga] place had been given up because it was found to be in the fly belt."[3] In 1905 Fr. Moreau took the approval of the company to obtain a permanent site in Monze. The BSA Company official, R.T. Coryndon, a determined colonialist of the type of Cecil Rhodes, was happy with the decision.

After making some progress, the Catholic Fathers wanted to go back to Southern Rhodesia to brief the higher authorities there. Before leaving, the Fathers asked Chief Monze to entrust three or four young boys to them for training. These native boys would be educated at Chishawasha in Southern Rhodesia, on the understanding that they would return with the Fathers when a permanent mission was set up. The Chief consented to the proposal on August 15, 1902. The boys were: Haatontola, Jahaliso, Bbinya, and Jojo. Haatontola was the son of Chief Monze's sister. He was considered to be a possible successor of Monze. Jahalisho, aged 16, was the right-hand man of Monze. Bbinya, a favorite son of Monze, was very intelligent. Jojo, the youngest of the four, aged 12, was a son of a man of the Monze's village. The boys themselves were eager and fully prepared to accompany. The Chief told Fr. Moreau what animal food was tabooed to each of them. He then asked the Father to teach them well and bring them back as soon as a mission could be opened in his territory. Thus a link between the Catholic Church and the Batonga was forged to the satisfaction of all parties, including the Chiefs and headmen of Monze and Kalomo areas. The seed of the Monze-Chikuni Mission was sown. It would be another two and a half years before the decisive step of opening the mission would be firmly taken.

Upon his return to Southern Rhodesia, Fr. Moreau reported, "We spent three days looking for a convenient site for this mission station." He added that at Chikuni, he had found a place which had good prerequisites: land, wood, water, and especially a large population nearby. There were four well-populated villages Syantumbu, Ufwenuka, Cobe, and Manya. A little far away were the other villages: Basanje, Cisuwo, Cizibwa, Syanamaila. Fr. Moreau stated,

> The headman of the nearest Krall is a good sort, progressive, anxious to learn and better his education. The land is good for cultivation and the rivers, though not perennial streams, flow during the greater part of the year. Firewood is abundant, and best of all, the inhabitants seem favorably disposed. We are erecting a temporary building and from this base, we shall explore the surrounding country. We can get fresh meat in abundance and cheap; I paid only 7 shillings for a sheap.[4]

Writing a month later, Fr. Moreau stated,

> The headman of the Krall, a thousand yards from us called Shiyamtumbu is very friendly. He usually appears in European clothers, trousers, coats and even shoes; when told we wanted to teach the people, he at once said he would be the first to learn; in fact, he has come everyday to put himself under Fr. Torrend's tuition and is determined to learn and read.

It was reported further: "Fr. Torrend engages young boys to help him in the garden; when tired, he makes them sit down and tell the nursery tales of the poeple in which he finds their moral code and history."

On July 14, 1905, the Catholic missionaries finally settled on the bank of the small Chikuni River. The Tonga farmers gave him oxen. Father Moreau had a good Oliver Plough. Within a few years. Father Moreau had 50 trained oxen and about 300 acres of land. The missionaries were by now fully accepted by the local people. The four Batonga boys were assured by the missionaries that the whites would not take away their cattle, but would help them achieve better life on earth and also prepare for the next. The Chikuni Mission at Chikuni was a good example of co-operation and progress toward the creation of centers of education and welfare. The Mission had some success from the beginning because of its open appeal to the people. The missionary penetration into the area had been the work of European missionaries in Southern Rhodesia. This essay takes note of the positive aspects of the missionaries whose influence has been great and impressive. In order to know the history of the district one has to know well the history of Chikuni Mission which had greatly contributed to the various developments of the area. Thus in principle the Tonga chiefs and men accepted the utility of a new code of morals and ethics. In this cultural encounter, the Western values dominated.

One hundred and fifty bricks were locally made and the foundation stone was laid in 1911. In 1912 the first Brother permanently appointed to Chikuni mission arrived. He was Brother John Masterson. Father Moreau realized the importance of education for the African women. He wished to have the Sisters of Notre Dame at Chikuni. The first task was to build a convent for the Sisters. Within a few months, the Sisters arrived and opened classes. About 200 Tonga girls and women were enrolled. In 1921, a large school room with a house for the priest was built at Chipembere village which was six miles north-east of Chikuni. At the request of Chief Monze, a large building was established to house the Catholic priests. "Out schools" were also opened at Singonya and Choompa. To train school teachers, St. Joseph School was opened in 1926. Out of 287 pupils between 1926 and 1939, 38 obtained certificates.

Four Polish missionaries arrived at about the same time. One of them was Father Ladislaus Zabdyr who came to Chikuni in 1928. He translated many Polish hymns in Citonga, and adapted them for native singing. With the help of two Tonga boys, Father Torrend printed in 1930, a revised and enlarged version of a school primer originally composed in Citonga by Fr. Bick in 1922. An important work on hygiene, written by Fr. Moreau for the use of schools, was adopted by the educational authorities of the Chikuni Mission. Thus the Catholics contributed to the spread of Western education in and around Chikuni. In 1939 Father Moreau moved to a new site at Singonya village. Fr. Zabdyr, who had been appointed Religious Superior for the whole Mission in June, 1939, was also made local Superior of Chikuni. He often went across to give spiritual talks to the Notre Dame Sisters at Chikuni. In 1949, a Secondary School was set up at Chikuni. It was the first Catholic School in Northern Rhodesia. Also was opened a Higher Teacher Training School.

Father Torrend lent Christian virtues to the area. Arriving in 1925, this untiring worker taught Citonga to the pupils as well as to the newly arrived missionaries. He died 1932. Likewise, Father Zabdyr addressed pupils on various topics of general interest. He talked about the virtues of Christian marriages and behavior. He dwelt on the usefulness of good and honest life.

The government was not entirely indifferent to the needs of the Mission. In 1943, the Chief Secretary Beresford Stokes, the District Commissioner of the Mazabuka Boma, and the Provincial Commissioner of Livingstone paid a visit to Chikuni. They were mainly interested in the development of agriculture. They saw four demonstration plots of the missions. They showed a keen interest in the grinding mill, the industrial work, in the Girls' School, and the recreation center. They promised the erection of a cement bridge over the Magoye stream.

In January 1948, Fr. Moreau, the main pillar of the Chikuni Mission, died. He was buried beside the grave of Fr. Torrend. Having come to Africa in 1885, he spent most of his life in the service of the Tongas. He had never retired. His funeral was a spontaneous tribute of Tonga people's gratitude to the grand old friend. He used to discourage every form of paternalism and patronage. He maintained that the initiation rites at the age of puberty should not be condemned unreservedly but be considered as stages which would naturally be passed as soon as others are reached. He further said, "Out of a sense of duty towards his deceased brother's wife, he feels obliged to raise the seed to the brother. Through Christian influence the African can be led to accept the missionaries word that such conduct is contrary to Christian law."

From some scattered sources we reasonably derive some idea about the nature of the African people. One mission record maintains, "They are simple and docile. They are a peaceable race." Elsewhere in the same source we note that "the girls are vain... on the crown they fasten and cap of cowry shells or breads. Women and girls carry pounds of brass wire round the ankles, and necks; and any scrap of iron they pick up is converted into an ornament." The source adds, "The boys are often neglected; their lot is hard one; in the early morning they have a drink of sour milk and then go out to herd; they return at sunset, and get their one meal; they sleep with the sheep and goats in a leaky hut." From these observations we may conclude that the Tonga girls were plain and simple as any other tribal girls. The boys were hard working and had to work in the field almost all day; life was not easy.

The contribution of the Chikuni Mission should not be underestimated. First, they introduced Western education which was essential to material progress. Second, the missionaries allowed the African to work in responsible positions. Yet it is equally true that the missionaries did not easily recruit priests and clergy from the Africans. Third, the missionaries tried to remove some of the harmful traditions in a moderate way. The over-all impression is that the missionaries have become the part of the social life of Monze. It is easy to criticize the missionaries for many of their genuine faults, yet one has to admit that the missionaries at Monze helped the process of modernization in agriculture and home economics. The history of the district is incomplete without recording the work of missionaries.

Monze Diocese

The Catholic Diocese of Monze comprises of the Southern Province with the exception of the city of Livingstone. The border of the Diocese ends in Zimba to the south. To the north-eastern area it includes Itezhi which is across the Kafue. The Diocese got its name from the place where the Bishop resided, Monze.

There are eighteen parishes in the Diocese of Monze: Monze town, St. Mary's Monze, Chilalantambo, Chirundu, Chikuni, Chivuna, Choma, Fumbo, Kafue Gorge, Kalomo, Kasiya, Lusito, Maamba, Mazabuka, Nakambala, Namwala, Siavonga, and Itezhi. Parishes are former "Missions." A parish is a sub-division of the Diocese. It is an area under the jurisdiction of a priest who is called a "Parish Priest." Priests working under him are called "Assistant Parish Priests" or "Curates." The Parish Priest is immediately responsible to his Bishop.

In each Parish in Monze district there are varying numbers of places where religious Mass is said. These places are known as

Mass Centres, grass roots of mission activities. Mass Centres are sub-divisions of a Parish where there are sufficiently large concentration of Catholics to merit having Mass at regular periods. In Monze there are the following Mass Centres: Monze Town, Zambia College of Agriculture, Monze Secondary School, Sigubbu, Mtaamba, Keemba Hill, Mandondo, Luyaba, Savoury's Farm. In St. Mary's there are the following Mass Centres: St. Mary's, Maamba, Haamapande, Sinundwe, Namilongwe R.R. Centre, and Rusangu Secondary School.

Within most of the parishes there are institutions run by the Catholic Church which do not come immediately under the jurisdiction of the Parish Priest. For instance, St. Kizito Pastoral Centre which was set up as a Catechists' Training Centre in 1967 under the able leadership of Fr. Keenan and which became a pastoral center in 1975, is not under the jurisdiction of the St. Marys Parish although physically it is within that area. The same situation exists for other Parishes, such as Monze Homecraft Centre, Monze Hospital.

There are different types of priests in the Diocese. Some priests are called Diocesan or Secular Priests and these are ordained for a particular diocese and are directly under the authority of the Bishop. There are also priests called Religion Priests who belong to different congregations of communities, i.e., the Jesuits, the Holy Ghost Fathers, the Bethlehimites, etc. These are loaned to the Bishop to work in the Diocese either in Parishes or institutions. They are directly under the head of their religious congregation. However, the Bishop may not reassign them to other work without the express permission of their own Provincial.

The Monze Diocese had always been involved in developmental projects to raise the standard of living of the Africans. In many of its parishes the Parish Priests, Sisters, Catechists and lay leaders ran projects such as Savings Clubs, Farmers' Clubs, Credit Unions,

Women's Clubs, draining of land, digging of wells, building of dams, school-leavers' projects and some small industries like the jam making and vegetable planting. There was one office responsible under the Bishop for all these Church development activities in the Diocese. It was called the Promoter for Development.

Wherever Mass was said, the local Catholics formed Church Councils which were responsible for the day to day running of Church at that particular center. The Parish Councils were made up of representatives from various Church Councils in a Parish. For example, there were six Mass Centres in St. Mary's Parish. Each of these had their own Church Council. Two representatives from each of these centres formed the Parish Council of St. Mary's Parish which, with the priest, were responsible for all Church affairs in the Parish.

Catholic Church at Monze

In July, 1959, the Catholic Church at the centre of Monze township was opened and blessed by the Most Rev. Adam Kozlowiecki, S.J., the Archbishop of Lusaka. Monze was still in the Lusaka Arch Diocese. In July, 1960, houses for the priests were completed and Fr. Denis O'Connell, S.J. was the first resident priest of Monze. Fr. C.O. Riordian, S.J. the Education Secretary, also lived in Monze with Fr. O'Connell.

In January, 1961, Monze became a separate Parish from the well-known Chukuni Mission. The Most Rev. Dr. James Corboy, S.J. was consecrated the Bishop of Monze in June, 1962. Monze became an independent diocese and was no longer under the Archbishop of Lusaka. A Diocesan Education Secretary also remained at Monze to supervise the working of the primary schools. He regulated the workings of the primary schools attached to the Monze Diocese. Later in the same year, the new Bishop took residence in Monze. Normal Parish work was continued all the time.

The Church at Monze had been involved in a lot of developmental work. In December, 1964, work began for the construction of the Monze Hospital. In subsequent years more wards and departments were added to the hospital which introduced Western hygiene and medicine. In 1966, the Homecraft Centre was established. This center was for teaching better methods of child care and cooking. It conducted residential courses. In 1970, the construction of the Nursing School began. Attached to it there was a School of Midwifery. In 1973 Red Devils' Youth and football team started for the senior youth of the town. The Football Team is still in existence. A garden was set up for the members of the club. The garden was later discontinued. In 1977 a Carpentry School was established for the Grade Seven "drop outs." It is situated in the old Mulumbwa School building. A more successful school of dressmaking was started for the girls. This was situated in different places but it is at present operating in the Homecraft Centre.

Thus Africans were introduced to various skills of the West. In most centres there are at present villagers working side by side with the Europeans. Monze hospital served the interests of many villages in the district. The missionaries had done more work in this respect than the government. The mission activities were shinning examples of dedication and co-operation. The local people had all the praise for the missionaries.[5]

Anglican Church

A good source of information for the reconstruction of the history of the Anglican Church is the private collection of two European farmers in Monze. George Atkins and his sons kept several important documents in two boxes in their farm house near

Monze. The Reverend Whitehead of Lusaka provided some useful information too. Several Church goers also contributed to the reconstruction of this history.

In 1905, the Europeans at Fort Jameson (Chipata) asked the Anglican Church for a priest. Since there was no Anglican Church in Northern or eastern Rhodesia, they wrote to the Bishop of Nyasaland. The Universities Mission to Africa (UMCA) was founded as a mission to Africans and was unwilling or unable to help because of its constitutional regulations. So the request went to another Anglican Society, the Society for the Propagation of the Gospel in Foreign Parts (SPG). This Society agreed to support a "Chaplain" to Europeans at Fort Jamesonn and one was appointed in 1905. The Europeans then built the present Saint Paul's Church in Chipata which was consecrated in 1906.

In 1910, as a Jubilee celebration of its fifty years' of existence, the UMCA founded the Diocese of Northern Rhodesia. The Bishop chosen was a former priest and doctor who worked in Malawi. He spoke Chinyanja, one of Malawi's main languages. He made an appeal in Malawi for priests and teachers to join him in Northern Rhodesia. One or two teachers came with him when he arrived at Livingstone in Northern Rhodesia. The first Malawian priest was Father Leonard Kamungu, who was also a volunteer. He came to Northern Rhodesia in 1911, and was posted to a station in the Eastern Province, but died in 1914, probably of food poisoning. The first Bishop died in 1913 for health reasons.

The missionaries brought some masons to Northern Rhodesia and built a stone church at Mapanza in the Southern Province called St. Bartholomew. It is about sixty miles from Monze. Thus missionaries began to appear in the Monze area with increasing hope of setting up permanent settlements. Toward the end of the nineteenth century the Monze area was served by two railway mission priests who came from Bulawayo in Southern Rhodesia.

In 1928, Bishop Alston May decided to concentrate all teachers training from the four missions stations at one central place, Fiwila Mission. St. Mark's College was opened there. It moved in 1930 to Mpanza, where it is now a secondary school. The headmaster was recruited from Malawi.

One source suggests that "for over thirty years Anglican Church services have been held in Monze in the hotel, the court house, private houses, railway coaches, etc." A Monze farmer named J. Owen-Wallen gave an acre of land near the township to the church in 1955. Services were offered monthly by Railway Missioners from the South African Railway Mission in Bulawayo. There was an African Church, St. Matthews, in the compound. An African Catechist was paid as pastor to the African Christians. The Railway Missioner took a communion service in English in the Old Court House, and then one for the African at St. Matthews. A public meeting was held at Monze at the government court house on April 20, 1955, to discuss the construction of a permanent building. Members present were G. Atkins, Sr., J. Blyth, Major L.J.E. Bucklan, G.P. Burdett, Brigadier G.A.L. Farewell, F. Ruddle. The Rev. S.T. Easter was an ex-officio member. It is clear that no African took any part at the initial stage of the construction of the Church building. The committee discussed the site of the church. J. Owen-Wallen offered a piece of land for the church. Two possible sites in the town were discussed. After full examination, it was decided by the general committee to leave the matter of selection to the organizing committee. Instructions included: (a) drawing up a plan for the building; (b) formulation of a scheme to raise funds. The organizing committee first met on May 13, 1955. The committee reported back in 1957. Under the chairmanship of Brig. G.A.L. Farewell, it proposed that the new church could also be used by the Africans. It was resolved that a letter should be sent to the Bishop of Northern Rhodesia concerning the trusteeship of funds and the church. In September, 1959, the Bishop of Northern Rhodesia wrote from Lusaka, the capital of Northern Rhodesia, that it was difficult to have freehold land for the churches. Then the Archbishop of Canterbury tried to persuade the colonial secretary to give freehold land for the Cathedral at Lusaka and failed. It was proposed that a ninety-nine year lease should be obtained to by-pass the legal obligations. It was agreed that there should be an individual approach to cases dealing with the use of the building by other religious bodies. The committee under the chairmanship of Farewell suggested that Africans could use the church building for services. Two hundred dollars was collected toward the construction of the building. The District Commissioner of Mazabuka refused to offer any funds. A "Jumble Sale" was organized in 1958 to raise funds. Murphy Construction was given the contract to build the Anglican Church.

There was some controversy regarding the naming of the church at Monze. There was no African participation in the entire process of deliberations on the issue. The Bishop of Northern Rhodesia wrote in December, 1959, "I would ask you to consider the possibility of naming the church in honor of St. Martin. There is no other church in the Diocese with that name. You may remember that he was the soldier who became a Bishop and was famous for cutting his cloak in half with a sword in order to give warm clothing to one in need. All visitors to London and those who listen to wireless are familiar with the Church of St. Martin in Trafalgar Square in the centre of London." The white station master of Monze also supported the idea. Eventually it was decided to name it the St. Martin Church.[6]

St. Kizito Pastoral Church

This institution which is described today as a Pastoral Centre began in 1967 as the Catechists' Training Centre. Catechists are paid partly by the Bishop and partly by the local Catholic community for which they work. The Catechists' Training Centre was started in 1967 by the Bishop of Monze. The Director of the Centre and Trainer of the Catechist was Fr. F. Keenen. The location of the Centre is ten kilometers west of Monze town and very close to the residence and Court of Senior Chief Monze who in 1967 granted the land to the Bishop to be used for the purpose described above. When the prospective catechist came for training he brought also his wife and family for the two years. The wives were trained in home crafts and related matters.

Before the building of the Catechists' Training Centre, Mass had begun in several Centres within what is now called St. Mary's Parish. The area around St. Kizito was in those days served by priests coming either from Monze town or Chikuni; it was not a Parish in its own right. With the arrival of Frs. Brain Sharkey and Dennis O'Connell the area was made a parish in its own right called St. Mary's. This parish still exists today and includes six Mass Centres. The Catechists' Training Centre was thus an institution within the Parish. Also in those days, two Malawian Sisters arrived to help with the Training of the Catechists' wives. These were Srs. Serafina Banda and Juliana Agnes Banda. The former taught at the primary school built between the Centre and the Chief's residence while the latter was fully involved with the Catechists wives and also some local women.[7]

By 1975 eight years were spent in training Catechists and it was felt there were now enough in the Diocese. Moreover, the emphasis in the church had now begun to move from paid Catechists to voluntary teachers of religion. So at that stage it was decided to reopen the Centre, which was closed for the lack of the local support, as a pastoral Centre for the training needs of all the categories of people in the Church, laymen priests, brothers, sisters. The training given at the Center was very wide varying from the deepening of faith through retreats and days of prayer to the imparting of skills relating to leadership and community awareness programs. Subjects taught included: the psycho-social method of Adult Education, Tonga language studies church music, and family planning.[8]

Seventh-Day Adventist Church

W.H. Anderson of the American Seventh Day Adventist Church (SDA) made an exploratory visit to the Tongaland in 1903. When he visited Chief Monze, the Chief showed keen interest in having the missionaries. Anderson looked for a suitable site. He decided on a site about 17 km from the present day Monze town, because it was near the rail line being planned by the BSA Company. There was also a natural spring called "Tinta which would provide water for a large Tonga community living around. Water was required for commercial agricutural activities. The adventists also believed in practical training. Anderson was given 5,436 acres of land by Chief Monze. The station was opened on July 1, 1905 and a small primary school was started. The station was initially known as Barotse Mission until 1913 when it was remaned Rusangu. "Rusangu" was derieved from the word "musangu" which was the name of a large tree.

Over time, many people joined the SDA movement. Some were willing to teach in village meetings. The first outschool was started in 1907. By 1911, there were five. These were Bweengwa, Kazengula, Hufhuwa, Nteme and Munanga. By the time Anderson left Rusangu in 1920, he had establised 14 outschools. The better peoples from the outschools were sent to Rusangu for further training. Before 1917, much of the teaching was in Zulu because Anderson's main assistant was a Zulu from Southern Rhodesia. Gradually, a Tonga teaching program opened at Rusangu.

Anderson paid attention to the village reconstuction in the

neighboring areas. His pupils gave instruction to the practical living in the local villages. He was replaced by S.M. Konigchen who served the mission until 1935. E.M. Mote followed and directed it until 1939. The colonial government wanted greater control over schools being run by various missions. The SDA then gave up control of many schools in the Monze district. Rusangu continued to stay under the SDA and imparted skills to hundreds of commercial farmers. It developed good health and practical development programs. The Adventists made a distinguished ground-breaking effort to bring development to the poeple of Monze district.

Njola Catholic Church

The Catholic Church at Njola in Chief Mwanza's area was set up in 1972, with the initiative of Father Frank O'Neill, S.J. who was aided by Nicholas Nduna and other local residents. Boys of Monze Secondary School made bricks with the help of the local people. The builders of the Diocese of Monze under the supervision of Br. Duune, S.J., constructed the nice building which stands near the gravel road, about four kilometers from the Chief Mwanza Palace.

The Njola Church, a sub-Parish, came under the Chivuna Parish which was part of the Diocese of Monze. Fr. O'Neill of Chivuna visited the sub-Parish once in a month but there were the local Catechist Philip Mwanza and other local leaders who looked after the mission which catered for the lay and religious needs of a large population. Many of the local people were Catholics. The Centre trained laymen to assume more and more responsibility for the development of the church.

Though the mission did not run any primary school in the area, it served the people in several ways. The money saved by the Credit Union was used for the purchase of fertilizers and seeds.

The Union had seven branches in the area. Mr. Rene and the Dutch volunteers helped by Mr. Robert regularly helped the local farmers. The Women Club, supported by the Church, offered training for nutrition courses. Twelve school leavers in 1978 had managed to form a Youth Club that made baskets and grew vegetables. The other two sub-Parishes were Nebukuyu and Kesako which were in Chief Mwanza's area.

There were several smaller Catholic churches near Njola. The small Moomba Church was at Namatabba. Its leader was John Hamalambo and Catechist was Peter Semende. The other church building was at Ntembo where the Catechist was Mathias Syagelika.[9] These churches were more interested in training rather than in conversion.

Endnotes

1 Chikuni Archives. Also interviews in 1977.

2 Zambezi Mission Records.

3 Papers at Chikuni Mission.

4 Archives at Catholic Church in Monze and Lusaka.

5 All information on the establishment of the Anglican Church was obtained from the farm house of Mr. Atkins, and the Office of the Church at Monze.

6 Papers at Atkins Farm at Monze.

7 From a Priest at St. Kizito.

8 Information supplied by Father Flannery, a teacher at Monze Secondary School.

9 The resident priest at Njola wrote most of the information for me.

Chapter V

SELECTION OF CHIEFS AND
TRANSFORMATION OF LOCAL AUTHORITY

Earlier we narrated the biographical sketches of chiefs in the Monze district. In this chapter we discuss the various responsibilities of chiefs, the succession process, as well as some related aspects of the local administration.

The District Secretary, the top civil servant in the district, had the right to attend meetings arranged for the selection of chiefs by the traditionalists. The District Secretary attended only to ensure impartiality and to record proceedings. He acted as a witness only.

When a chief was to be selected, the following procedure was followed:

1. Meetings for succession were held at places selected by the local leaders and were conducted according to the local customs. The meetings were not held in the Government District Headquarters. This was to ensure that the government officials did not take sides in the process.

2. When there was more than one candidate, the minutes of the meeting had to show that the claims of both or all parties concerned had been taken into account, and the reasons offered as to why any claim was disqualified and ignored. Where necessary a vote was taken. Thus there was an element of democracy.

3. The District Secretary present prepared a family tree based on the information provided and obtained from the Boma records. He relied on several individuals for this. This genealogy was used by the District Secretary to find out if the candidate was the proper one.

The minutes of the meetings and the family tree were circulated among all present. This was to avoid any doubt as to the legality of the candidate.

Although he did not take any active role in the selection of the chiefs, the District Secretary had some responsibilities to assign specific duties to the chiefs. There was mutual trust. The chiefs were given the following work:

1. Chiefs were to follow their traditional customs and manners provided they did not contradict the British imposed laws. In cases of any contradiction the British law prevailed.

2. Chiefs were to report to the District officials in cases of famine and spread of diseases.

3. Chiefs were the natural guardians and protectors of the people under their authority.

The administration was conducted with the help of elders and councilors. Traditionally, Chiefs' duties included the following as well:

4. Chiefs were leaders in defence against raids by stronger hostile neighbors. Cooperation from all members of the society was the essence.

5. Settlement of simple and ordinary disputes was in accordance with the tribal rules and ethics and the strong common sense upon which people had faith. Nobody disputed the decision.

6. As rain-makers the chiefs offered prayers. Only a chief could organize a royal hunt annually. None would doubt the supposed inherent quality of the chief as a rain-maker, although there might be no rain at all after prayer.

7. Since land could not be alienated, chiefs had the responsibility to allocate land. In doing so, the chiefs consulted the elders. The ownership of land was communal. Any allotment of land did not mean the transference of actual ownership to any particular owner.

8. Individually as traders they exchanged goods in a barter

system within their localities. The chiefs had no monopoly of trade. It was a kind of free market. There was virtually no economic regulation imposed by the Chiefs.

The colonial administration had expanded the role of the chiefs in the interest of modernization. The chiefs had become more important in the sense that they were involved in many affairs. A Chief or Senior Chief was given the responsibility to form village productivity committees. In a circular dated November 5, 1971, President Kenneth Kaunda stressed the need to mobilize masses for the reconstruction of economy. He wrote thus:

> ...these are changing times. So the role of institutions [chiefs] will also change. Our needs are changing. New problems and challenges have arisen. To resolve new problems and challenges we cannot depend upon old instruments alone; we have to find new ones and also sharpen the old.

The idea was clear. The chiefs must participate in building dams and bridges. They had to recruit voluntary labor. Mere maintenance of law and order in his area was not enough. Any local participation meant less delay in the completion of the projects. With this goal in mind, the Village Registration and Development Act was passed by the Zambian National Assembly.

Sections 18 and 19 of the Village Registration and Development Act indicate that the chiefs were allowed to address the Ward Development Committees. They would ensure that Productivity Committees were set up to promote friendship and coordination. They would give priority to establish small industries and work for improvement in agriculture. Government officials used to help them. Chiefs were asked to report to the District Secretary about the progress of local projects.

Side by side with the increased role of chiefs were the creation of new local institutions at the instances of the government. One such authority was the Plateau Tonga Native Authority, based in Monze township. The idea behind this creation was to get the active support of the local people in the running of a modern economic structure. Here the people's participation was more important. The Constitution of the Plateau Tonga Authority was as follows:

Members: The District Commissioner; All chiefs in the area.

Staff: The Chief Executive Officer; The Treasurer; the Administrator. The administrator was the day to day manager whose duty was very wide.

Ministry: Provincial Local Government Administration.

Clerical Staff: The clerk; the typist; drivers.

Functions:

1. To grant loans for various purposes.
2. To establish public transport system.
3. To impose certain levies on the local community.
4. To appoint an Alderman.
5. To provide pension for the employees.
6. To take legal action if necessary.
7. To maintain market places.

From these it would appear that the developmental work was being handed to the local people. This was not indirect rule but the system of local administration. The functions of the Authority were:

1. To make loans and grants of money to local people for certain projects, such as bridges and schools. Local hospitals were subsidized by the government.

2. To impose by-laws and levies. Levies were imposed on bridges.

3. To establish public transport services. Here chiefs were involved in building roads. There was no coercion in recruiting labor. Small wooden bridges were to be constructed on creeks and tunnels.

4. To establish markets; these markets were open and catered for the local needs. Market women sold their produce in the market but they had to obtain a permit and pay a license fee to the local authorities.

5. To act as licensing authority for traders doing business in the Monze markets.

The composition of the Plateau Tonga Authority demonstrates that the public of the area were directly given authority in the running of their local affairs. Working for the Provincial Local Government Administration, this Authority appointed its own Chief Executive Officer and the Treasurer. In the absence of regular auditing there were cases of embezzlement.

Between 1964 and 1965 the central government introduced more agencies to the district. The District Local Government Authority was created. This was separate from the office of the District Secretary. The loss of control over the local authority was a major reduction in the power of the District Secretary. It created conflicts between the District Secretary and the District Local Government Officer. Ironically, it reduced the role the former District Commissioner, now the District Secretary, in the policy making decision concerning the economic development. Now the Native Authority became the guiding and controlling agency in local affairs. The District Commissioner could persuade the Native Authority to embark on some development projects such as building sheltered markets or new school buildings. But the District Secretary could no longer do this after 1965 when the District Local Government Officer took over. Also, the quality of the District Secretaries proved to be lower after independence of Zambia. In fact the civil servants in the district did not always look to the District Secretary for guidance. Other officials became involved in economic and social projects.

Development in the economic field became the key word in the late 1950s and 1960s. Besides the institutions of chiefs and local authorities, there were set up other agencies to cover areas not administered by the earlier institutions. These new establishments were mostly related to agriculture and its problems. One such organ was the Northern Rhodesia African Farmers Union with its headquarters in Monze. The aims and objectives of the Union were to create a spirit of co-operation and understanding among African farmers in Northern Rhodesia for the mutual benefits. Other goals were:

(a) To foster the high standard in stock farming, and to promote integration of livestock and crops in order to achieve agricultural stability;

(b) To represent African farming members of the Union in negotiations with the Government including Native Authorities;

(c) To promote matters contributing to African Agricultural welfare and prosperity;

(d) To foster the protection of natural resources.

Membership of the Union was open to all farmers; there was a membership fee. The Union used to get donations also.

It is admitted that there was economic expolitattion during the colonial period in Zambia. Indeed, Central Africa was meant to supply the raw material needs of the mother country, Britain, is clear and the history of this has been recorded by many historians. Zambian nationalists complained that very little was done to industrialize the area. Yet it is equally true that the colonial administration made every effort to increase local productivity for the good of the people. The subsistence base of the local economy was difficult to change because most people were satisfied with their produce and there was the lack of capital. Efforts were made by the colonial agents and from these modest beginnings the independent government of Zambia after 1964 introduced substantial changes in the economy and the society.

The chiefs' role had recently been extended in the district. Referring to the theft and buying of cattle, Chief Chona pointed out several issues. The small police force at Monze town could not cope with the cattle theft and as such chiefs themselves took up the responsibility of protecting animals. Many buyers came from far away places to purchase cattle. It was difficult to know their identity. In a meeting in August, 1977 Chief Chona called upon the head men to minimize the loss of cattle through theft. The matter was discussed and the following were resolved through a consensus.

1. Any one wishing to sell an animal must, together with the buyer, see the head man and show the animal to the head man.

2. When the buyer wants to get a permit from the Chief, he must drive all the animals to him to be seen. He must also bring his National Registration Card.

3. No seller would do the transaction without the knowledge of the Chief.

Likewise, the chiefs had to take up new obligations and duties to help the government variously without any remuneration. For instance, Chief Chona reminded the people in a written circular that every new child should be registered with the Government Registrar. A parent had to pay twenty-five ngwee for the registration.

The Courts

The court system in Zambia comprised the Supreme Court, the High Court, subordinate magistrates' courts, and local courts, all of which had both original criminal and civil jurisdiction. The basis of jurisprudence in all courts, aside from the local courts, consisted of English common law. The statutes still in force originated in the colonial and federation periods (1953–1963), and also the Acts passed by the Zambian legislature based in Lusaka. The local courts dealt mainly with customary law, although they had certain additional statutory powers.

The highest court was the Supreme Court, which heard only appeals from the High Court. It had a Chief Justice, a Deputy Justice, and two Supreme Court judges, all appointed by the President. When sitting as a court of appeal it was required to be composed of an uneven number of judges, no fewer than three.

Judges and magistrates, except Supreme Court judges, were appointed by an independent Judicial Service Commission and were removable only by that commission for proven misbehavior or inability to perform duties due to physical reasons. The commission consisted of the Chief Justice as chairman, one judge of the High Court, the chairman of the Public Service Commission, and one presidential appointee who must be either a judge or a former judge. Although the courts continued to be formally independent, they had no real power to protect the Constitution from legislative or executive interference. Over the years they have become responsive to the values of the political system of which they were a part.

The gradual Zambianization of the courts began in 1969. By early 1979 most judges were Africans. The Magistrate court at Monze performed both civil and criminal cases. But even today minor disputes are settled by the elders of the villages and people have good faith in the process. Of course, with the introduction of western education, the educated Africans took most cases to the government court at Monze.

Chapter VI

MARRIAGE PATTERNS AND DIVORCES

The word "family" among the Tonga refers not so much to the nuclear family of husbands, wives, and children but to an extended family that includes several generations. In rural areas this group consisting of all the heirs of a living elder may be the corporate property-holding unit, the co-operative work group, the sphere of shared cooking and eating. Polygyny is traditionally permissible but not universally found. Polygynous households in the past were generally those of important chiefs. Chiefs often needed additional women because of the social obligations including the food preparation, beer brewing, and the cultivation of most crops. Chiefs also frequently used marriage as a way of building political alliances. Before 1964 statutory marriages were for whites and customary marriages for blacks. Very few Africans had chosen to marry under statutory law. In this chapter, I discuss traditional marriages and divorces. Most villagers do not go to the Marriage Register to complete the legal process. They prefer to marry in the traditional way. Those who go for marriage registration have to pay a fee of two Kwacha in the presence of two witnesses.

Marriage Patterns

The noted American scholar Elizabeth Colson has recognized three main groups among the Tonga people. These are the Plateau Tonga, who live in the northern part of the plateau; the valley or Gwembe Tonga; and the Southern Tonga or Toka. They have almost identical marriage and social customs.

As the girl approached puberty she was trained for her future role in the family. There was a period of seclusion during which a ceremony was observed. This ceremony marked the girl's maturity.

Among the Tonga the girls got a new name to show their new adult status. She was called "Kamwale."

The prospective husband had to pay bride-money to the family of the girl. He usually paid cattle for his wife. At Monze some men used to pay two cattle and some garments. The husband went to his wife's village, gave presents and brought her back to his village. Then they set up their own household. Once settled, the man had the right to look for a second wife. The first wife would not object to this because polygyny was considered as a social security. More children meant that at least some would survive to perform the family sacrifices. Secondly, the man was not supposed to sleep with his pregnant wife. Thirdly, more wives would mean more hands for work in the maize and vegetable fields.

The new wife had her own house or room, her own pots and pounding stick. She got her own gardens as well. Many women liked their husbands to have several wives because that meant less work for each of them. So in the rural areas of Monze, polygyny was very common. The chiefs and the village head men had several wives. The Tonga living near the rail line did not favor polygyny. I asked almost all the Zambian teachers of Monze Secondary School and found that they had no second wife. They argued that polygyny was uneconomic.

Divorce Settlements

In spite of many common features, there were some specific reasons for divorce among the Monze Tonga. The following cases were obtained from the records of the First Class Magistrate (Mr. Paul Mwanga) at Monze where cases from the interior were brought for trial. The litigants were not educated elite, nor were they rich farmers. They were typical tribal people with all the traditional beliefs.

1970. Edward vs. Esther (Chief Monze)

Esther, was the only wife of Edward who was a small subsistence farmer cultivating maize in his field. She argued that she had "lived well with my [her] husband from 1964 to 1967." The wife accused the husband of not sleeping in her house from 1967. Moreover, Edward, apparently an innocent man, did not give her clothes and garments. The wife thus concluded that the husband did not love her any more. The judge asked her if there was any pecuniary problem, or monetary difficulties. The wife answered in the negative. Witnesses were few and even the parents of the parties were not brought to court, which was set up by the government with its own clerk of the court. The Magistrate, Paul Mwanga, had good experience both in tribal and modern systems of divorce settlements.

The husband was asked to respond in person and he did that by offering his side of the divorce case. Edward said that his "wife was running with other man."

The proceedings were recorded in detail. The complaint was read to the litigants. Several headmen were present during the hearing which lasted for several weeks. The parties did not employ lawyers. The magistrate had to rely on the issues raised rather than any broad constructive approaches. He believed that the cases could be decided by the facts offered at the court by the persons present. He eventually gave the judgment for the divorce on the merit of both the partners' arguments. The wife soon left the husband's village for the parent's home. The separation was legalized.

1973. Thereza vs. Valentene (Chief Ufwenuka)

It was an appeal case coming from the lower court at a village not far from Monze town. The lower courts record was not available. As it appeared from the First Class Magistrate Court, one party complained of cruelties by the husband. The wife argued that the husband was "cruel" to her. Asked by the Magistrate what was meant by cruelties, the wife responded by saying that the husband, a young man of 27, used to assault her "for no apparent reason."

The husband told the court that he did not know that it was an offence to beat the wife. He declared, "I assaulted her because when I came to the house from beer drinking with friends and neighbours, I found her out."

The wife favored the divorce because her husband did not divorce his other wife. It appears that the wife relied on the assumption that any physical abuse was against the principle of marriage. On the other hand, the husband believed that it was his duty to "fix" the wife in her proper place; beatings were part of the daily routine in cases of any deviation. There was nothing wrong because, he felt, the husband had the superior moral right to correct the irregular behavior of his own wife.

The Magistrate at Monze followed this line of argument and gave the judgment for the divorce. The separation was almost instant.

1975. Shadreck vs. Anne (Chief Mwanza)

In this case the parties argued over sexual morality. Extra-marital relations were involved and both the husband and the wife accused each other of insincerity.

Briefly stated, the self-employed Shadreck, who had some education, brought the case to the court to accuse his wife of adultery. He declared that the wife had a boy friend. So the husband chased her out from the house. Now he sought divorce.

The Magistrate agreed with the argument of the husband and granted the divorce.

1977. Ester vs. Solomon (Kaimba village)

Divorce was sought due to the ill-treatment of the wife by the husband. She stated, "He usually fights me." The Magistrate granted the divorce.

These selected cases from different chiefdoms in Monze district point to the nature of general disputes arising out of misunderstandings. It appears that the wife did not get enough recognition from the court. The voice of the husband carried more weight in general. The husbands tended to win. Loose morals were cited and in most cases wives were found to be at fault. Only occasionally high-handedness of the husbands could be counted as responsible for the divorce.

From the court cases it is clear that both husbands and wives brought cases for divorce. Relatives of the husbands supported the husbands' position, while relatives of wives supported her daughters' line of argument. Witnesses from outside the families were brought, examinations were held and the court in most cases granted divorce. Only rarely was a divorce prevented. At times, the court made arrangements for a good-behavior period after which the cases might come up if the husband and wife did not reconcile. In a case brought from Ufwenuka's area, the wife pleaded that the husband failed to honor the agreement and still assaulted the wife. The court granted the divorce. One thing seemed to be socially acceptable – the beating of a wife by her husband. Elizabeth Colson admits that in the valley, the Tonga are well aware that "divorce is a possibility throughout the years that a marriage lasts."[1]

Apparently divorce in the area seems to be an easy affair. In order to obtain the traditional view about divorce, I went to see several chiefs and councilors to identify the nature of marriage bond in the traditional setting. My findings seem to be contrary to conventional wisdom.

The seemingly easy break-up of the marriage bond in a traditional society may be explained by the prevalence of the utility notion of marriage itself divorced from intimacy and love. Yet this should not divert the investigators from the reality of a reconciliatory approach which might be detected in a settlement of marital disputes. There is a general desire not to break up the marriage so easily. In a few cases, mostly on appeal, the Monze court took a stand to save the marriage. As I talked to the Chief Magistrate at Monze, he remarked that the interest of the individual could be balanced against the social interest served by other elements in the society of social welfare and these elements include the preservation of marriage. There were also house meetings which settled differences. In most cases, wives got most of the advice and harsh criticism.

Commenting on "Social Control and law in Africa," the Ottenbergs write, "There is an attempt not only to arrive at a settlement but frequently to reconcile the parties [in marital disputes] concerned, so that they can live at peace in the future – an important aspect of societies whose members live in close contact with one another."[2] They suggest that the middle range societies, culturally homogeneous and autonomous, are formed almost on the basis of kin ties while some societies emphasize residential and association groups. In such cases, the group identification is very important in maintaining order and in guiding individual behavior. Extra-legal devices settle disputes.

Since marriage is seen as an alliance between the kin groups of husband and wife as well as a union between individuals, several factors act as preventives against a break in marriage. For instance, a wife's kinsmen have to return a substantial number of cattle to her husband before she can be freed from marital ties. This direct proprietary interest of the parents is expected to urge the daughter toward the reconciliation of differences with the husband, while the husband is guided, principally, by his material interest. In explaining the bond of marriage, the Sociologist Southall notes that in subsistence societies the marital roles of spouses are deeply embedded in a widely ramifying system of formally structured kinship relationships."[3] In Zambia, a typical example of middle range societies, there has been a trend toward the preservation of marriage as a social institution. Zambia is an example of what Southall calls "subsistence societies."[4] With this subsistence economy the tribal people demonstrate what Service calls "social reciprocity," in the marriage transaction. Thus a supreme effort is made to save a troubled marriage.[5] In fact one should know the process of reconciliation before passing a valid judgment.

The neglected wife at first reports to her parents. The husband also sends a message to his parents-in-law informing them of the dispute. Even if the daughter explained that her husband mistreated her, the father would back up the husband at the initial stage, and ask the daughter to go back to the husband's house. If the girl does not return at once, then he would instruct his wife to take her daughter back to the house. On reaching the daughter's home, the mother-in-law would tell the son-in-law that she has brought his wife who has run away from him. The son-in-law would give her clothes in appreciation. The wife's family, in particular, would keep an eye on the progress of the marriage. Levi-Strauss offers a general explanation for this type of constructive approach. He maintains that from the societal point of view the women are "exchanged" for the mutual benefit of the kinship groups. This concept of social reciprocity helps the maintenance of the tribal marriage bond.[6]

Endnotes

1 The Chief Magistrate at Monze, Mr. Mwanga, handed over to me at least fifteen files relating to the marriage disputes. I returned the files to him and asked his permission if I could use them for my book. He allowed me to do so.

2 Simon and Phoebe, *Cultures and Societies in Africa* (New York: Random House, 1960), pp. 234–35.

3 Ibid., p. 344.

4 William A. Southall, *Social Change in Modern Africa* (Oxford: Oxford University Press, 1969).

5 Elan R. Service, *Primitive Social Organization: An Evolutionary Perspective* (New York: Random House, 1962), p. 123.

6 This summary is based on the reports obtained from several villages in Chief Monze. I witnessed several marriage disputes being settled in Monze.

Chapter VII

SOCIAL STRUCTURE IN MONZE AREA

Though some parts of Zambia are well urbanized, most areas of the Monze district are rural areas, which were the least affected by social and economic changes. Here the individual was a member of a household, an extended family, a village, a neighborhood, and in some cases, a clan, which was a formal political system of chieftainship. Each of these communities made their own demand on a person's behavior and offered him or her certain rules and obligations.

The majority of the Tonga farmers in the area were engaged in cash farming in which maize was predominant. Virtually all significant farmers farm maize. Sunhemp, groundnuts, velvet beans, cotton and some other commodities were raised for sale. Individual small farmers sold pigs, cattle, and poultry. Commodities were exchanged in the central market at Monze. Corrugated tin shelters were provided by the local council and market men and women paid rent.

The commercial farmers, or elite, could be easily identified. Years after independence in 1964, most commercial farmers on the line of rail produced for profit. Many of them came from Southern Rhodesia, or South Africa. Living near the rail lines these white farmers had a higher standard of living than that of the black farmers. These elite farmers had European furniture, mirrors, and utensils. Many of them had their own running water. In a way these commercial farmers lived in a world of their own. Some farmers had maize mills and saw mills. Most of them used tractors and motor vehicles. They had larger storage facilities. Both economically and socially, they were well placed in the midst of poor farmers.

It is interesting to note the social relationships among the people. It is not certain whether higher social order was based on wealth and color. However, certain features of social status could be noted. The Tonga in Monze usually followed a matrilineal system of descent. Until the coming of the whites, there were no hierarchies. In fact, there were no positions based on office or rank, although the rain-shrine keepers exercised a small influence. The basic fact is that every person was bound into a network of relationship with neighbors and with some people who lived further afield. Naturally there appeared no clear social higher order.

However, different types of kinship linkage carried specific duties and obligations which were approved by custom. A sisters son might inherit from his uncle, whereas his son did not. In day-to-day farming and domestic activities most links carried the same weight of obligations. These relationships did not create any inherent status.

The African commercial farmers were not dependent on any other head or homestead. Being rich, they were in a position to have a considerable number of homesteads dependent on them. Generally, the commercial farmers did not have as many dependent homesteaders as the resources would allow. It appears that it is the commercial farmers who did not allow such relationships to develop mainly because it was not sufficiently to their advantage.

Although commercial farmers did not form a larger number of relationships with their homesteaders, they maintained relationships with large numbers of people who lived in their homestead. In short, the commercial farmers belonged to a small but significant class of individuals. The skill of farmers was sought after by the non-commercial farmers.

Specifically, the model of relationship and the issue of social status can be explained well with reference to the following:

a. *Marriage and family.* Couples from dissimilar ethnic backgrounds generally married under customary law of the husband's group. Typical variations among the Tonga system of customary law included the amount and the recipients of bride wealth, and the bride service. Marriages had traditionally been based on practical rather than emotional grounds. Ethnic background, employment, site conditions, religious affiliation, and even friendship were likely to influence the settlement pattern in the area. No particular area was regarded as superior to other areas.

b. *Lineage*. A lineage could be defined as all those who acknowledged common ancestors through known links through either men in some areas, or women in other areas. Such lineages might consist of only a few generations. Lineages might function as corporate groups overseeing inheritance, settling disputes among their members and acting as political entities in competition with other such units. Powerful chiefs and powerful lineages were not necessarily alternatives.

c. *New economic grouping*. A type of an elite class developed due to the accumulation of wealth in some African hands. Members of the elite, usually came from poor families. For instance, Mr. Simuloka of Monze town, coming from a poor family background, rose to a new economic status by his hard work and intelligence. A secondary school graduate, and a owner of a butchery, Simuloka had considerable social and political status. He was elected councilor to the Monze township council in the 1970s and was associated with the work of the district governor. He used to preside over many social functions. His higher status was based on newly acquired wealth. He owned a large old Cadillac car.

It is interesting to note that President Kenneth Kaunda's government took certain steps to equalize opportunities. The government abolished in 1976 the more prestigious fee-paying, government-aided schools and medical facilities. At Monze, the elite retained family connections with the non-elite and social relationships were free from any inhibition. Thus no clear hereditary superior class developed at Monze.

Urban Tonga

The urban elite who used to own houses in Monze township were in mostly bureaucratic positions formerly filled by whites. The sub-elite at Monze township had skilled jobs in education, nursing, office work, etc., which were also originally filled by either Asians or Europeans. The sub-elites considered themselves a part of modern Zambia, with the wealthy elite, even though they lacked financial resources, big houses, and occasional cars. Those who were self employed in good, well-stocked shops or in commodity exchange warehouses were sub-elites. They had higher prestige than small traders and fishermen at the Monze open market.

Whites

Whites from South Africa and Southern Rhodesia had settled in Monze since the last decade of the nineteenth century. There are no statistics available for the white population in the district. However, on a broader scale, it is estimated that the white farmers of Southern and Central provinces, estimated at between 300 and 350, produced 40 percent of the staple crop, maize. In the Monze district it is well known that most of the effective farmers had been whites in the past. Before independence, the Whites working for the Zambia Railways had formed their own trade unions which were influential organs locally. This was, in a way, the beginning of an organized labor movement.

The managerial staff of both the Standard Bank and Barclay Bank at Monze were whites who were professionally trained. Socially they commanded high respect. Most Africans had to prove their financial eligibility to obtain loans. In almost all cultural celebrations, these whites used to be invitees who were seated in front benches in the assemblies. There seemed to be the continuation of colonial mentality in the sense that most whites commanded very high respect simply because they were whites. In the 1978 Independence Day celebration at Monze, peoples from distant places assembled. The front row chairs were occupied by the District Governor, the District Secretary, the white farmers and bank officials.

Asians

In and around the Monze town, Asians, consisting of about thirty families, had a higher social status than that of their black neighbors. Most Asians in the 1970s were Hindus, although a few Muslims traders lived in the town. Away from the town, in a smaller township called Chisekesi, there were two distinguished Greek families including Mr. Chavaras, who was a successful retail trader and wholesaler. These two families enjoyed much higher status than the majority of the neighboring Tongas. Asians in Monze were particularly prominent in the clothing industry. Such names as Kantu Bhai Patel, Jiwan Bhai Patel, J. Naik commanded high respect because of their charity, wealth, and amicable social behavior. Kantu Bhai Patel and others used to keep some Tonga children in their houses; they were given education and jobs and eventually commanded respect among the Tonga. Asians in Monze were also engaged in medicine, law, and education. Most of the Monze Government Secondary School teachers were Asians of diverse ethnic background, but collectively they were regarded as one group by the local people and were deservedly held in high esteem. Likewise, a few science and mathematics teachers in Chikuni Mission Secondary School were of Asian origins. The contribution of these Asian teachers and traders to the local economy was significant. Many of the Asians were Zambian citizens and had lived in the town for generations. In a way, it was a society where friendship and cordiality prevailed.

The Asians moved toward a common Anglophone Zambian elite culture. Earlier, in the 1960s the Hindu and Muslim communities maintained Gujrati and Koranic supplementary schools to socialize their children. One interesting thing is that many Asians lived in their extended family system, which was not very different from the Tonga system.

Socially, there appeared to be a hierarchical order in which the educated Tonga elite commanded high esteem. The whites and the Asians, because of their wealth and education, were held in high respect. Many of the Asians used to lend money to the local people who naturally showed respect to them. In short, a type of invisible class system prevailed in the district, although there existed no open class system.

In the late 1970s and early 1980s the Tonga commercial farmers at Monze belonged to a small but significant class of wealthy individuals. The Paulson family had a large cattle farm and milk from the farm was sold to the nearby boarding school. The family had a large maize farm in which tractors were used. After the departure of most of the Whites, Zambians bought their farms and became wealthy. But they lacked many of characteristics necessary for a elite group. They did not develop institutions of their own. They did not have pre-eminence, the corporate right.[1]

Endnotes

1 For further information see Irvin Kaplan, ed., *Zambia, A Country Study* (Washington D.C.: The American University, 1969); A.D. Jones, "Social Networks of Farmers Among the Plateau Tonga of Zambia," in P.C. Lloyd, ed., *The New Elites of Tropical Africa* (Oxford: Oxford University Press, 1966; Elizabeth Colson, *Marriage and Family Among the Tonga of*

Northern Rhodesia (Manchester: 1958); and Elizabeth Colson, *The Plateau Tonga of Northern Rhodesia: Social and Religious Studies* (Manchester: Manchester University Press, 1962).

Chapter VIII

LOCAL STORIES

I collected some stories from various sources in the district. They were partially written for me by interpreters such as Bruno Mwiinga. One method of collecting these stories was to ask an elderly man to narrate them and then verify the same from another man. In almost each village there were wise resource men whom I relied on. The stories were recorded in Tonga in the first instance. The translation was as literal as possible. This was to reconstruct the stories as much as possible in their true spirit. These stories reflected tribal social ethos and principles. By taking animals as characters the story teller has the advantage that they are comparatively unknown and their habits and forms are familiar but their inward life is not known. More imagination can be attributed to them. The story teller can keep up the names of the animals and then all the rest he can fill in out of his mind. He can conceive the animals doing the thing which we should deem out of all reason and from this he can pass into highly imaginative situations. In short he creates an ideal world.

1. The Hare and The Elephant (Chief Monze)

A long time ago there lived a powerful hare in an isolated place. The animal wanted to eat an elephant's meat. It did not know how to get an elephant and how to obtain its meat for eating.

One day he thought of a wise plan. He hung his axe in a big tree. Under it he dug out a big hole and put a spear inside its hole to deceive the elephant. He then made the top look like a natural thing.

When the hare saw the elephant coming, he began to cry. This drew the attention of the elephant and it came to the hare slowly to see what was wrong with the hare. The hare explained to the elephant that his valuable axe was caught up in the high tree and that he was unable to get it; he needed it badly. The elephant was filled with sympathy. He wanted to help the hare but as soon as he came under the tree, he dropped into the hole and the trick appeared to have done the expected work. The elephant died and the hare had plenty of meat to eat.

The lessons are: (a) perseverance can bring success; (b) wisdom can be found in small people, not only big fellows. A society that had only oral means to teach had to find out clever means to impart tribal ethos to the children. It was also a sign of intelligence. The elderly people who narrated these stories commanded respect. At the same time, children and adults were asked to consider several clever moves to obtain success. Success depended on the clever manipulation of conditions. The hare, being small, could kill an elephant, and so any lesser man could conquer the hostile conditions. The moral is that if men put all their heart into a desired thing, and if all energies are put into the thing to be done, then it can be done. The hare gained because of his perseverance and single-mindedness.

2. Marriage of the Chief's Daughter (Chief Chona)

I began with the Chief Chona himself who provided me with a brief story (in English) regarding the marriage plan of a chief's daughter. After noting down the story, I gathered some more information from a few headmen. Later on I read out my written version to my main interpreter, Bruno Mwiinga of the Monze Night School. He confirmed that the story as written by me conformed to the spirit of the story as heard from elders in the area.

Here again the story reflected the tribal social ethos. The story may be narrated as follows.

Once upon a time there lived a proud animal who had a very beautiful daughter who was to be given in marriage to the best male animal. The chief publicized the message in order to attract the people of the neighborhood. Naturally, many male animals came to the chief.

All of them brought so many gifts for the daughter that the chief could not decide. He then hit upon a plan to suit the wishes of every competitor. The boy animal had to drink boiling water from a pot in front of all people assembled so that there would be no complaint. Many tried to drink the boiling water but died. None could finish the boiling water and so the marriage was not performed.

At last, a clever male animal came forward with a clear idea. He asked the chief if he could bring all his relatives from his village so that more people would witness the drinking of water; the chief permitted. The clever animal, an hare, asked the chief whether he could show the boiling water to all relatives present. The chief allowed. The hare went around to all of his relatives one by one to demonstrate that the water was hot. The relatives were so many that by the time he went to the last relative the water got as cold as the water in a deep well. Then the hare went to the center of the place and drank all the water from the pot at ease. Every one congratulated him and relatives were happy. The happiest person was the chief who realized that his son-in-law was a strong man. So the hare married the girl.

The lessons of the story are: (a) A clever man can manage things even in front of a crowd; (b) A winning man has to be imaginative; (c) It is not easy to get a beautiful girl for marriage; one has to demonstrate his intelligence.

3. The Hare and the Hyena (Chief Ufwenuka)

In the remote past when the world was still young, the hare and the hyena used to live together in peace. One day the two decided to buy a cattle. The hare bought a cow and the hyena a bull. After some months they found a calf in the kraal. They began to quarrel as to whom the new born animal belong to. Each of them began to give explanations for his ownership. At the end they went to ask Mr.Fox to come and help them.

The Fox came and told them to wait and see where the calf would suck. The calf, of course, sucked from the mother. They all concluded that it was for the hare as he was the owner of the cow. The hyena went away with his bull.

One day the hare met the hyena with his bull in the bush. The hare was very frightened, thinking that the hyena would take revenge. He thought of a plan. He asked the hyena what name he had been given when the animal was born. The hyena told the hare his name. When asked what name the hare had been given, he said "I am Mr. Hyena Eater, and the one I will eat to-day is the third one." The hyena was very frightened and immediately ran away. He became so afraid of the hare that he decided to run away wherever he saw him.

The story came from a matrilineal society. It could be that it was told or invented by fathers (male factors) to show that even though the child came from the mother's womb, and sucked from her breasts, yet it was not only hers. Surely the bull in the story was partly responsible for the existence of the calf.

4. Hare and Elephant (Chief Choongo)

Once an hare told an elephant if he would like to play hide-and-seek. That would prove who was clever at the game. The elephant told the hare that he was more powerful and also more skillful at the game. Then the hare asked the elephant to hide. The elephant went into a distant place and shouted telling that he was hiding. The hare came and found him at once because the elephant was in the open. Then the hare told the elephant to remain there so that the hare could go to a new place to hide. He lay down at the bush, turned on his back, and said to the elephant to find him out. Since the hare was showing his eyes the elephant called the people to go there and see that the earth had eyes. The elephant proved to be a fool and the hare was the winner because he was more cunning.

The lesson of the story is that an humble person also can be a winner if can use his intelligence.

In conclusion, quoting from Smith and Dale, "It may be said in conclusion that man's common human-heartiness is in the tales. Grief and joy are shown to touch the same chords in their breasts as in ours. How simply, yet how touchingly, are the fundamental human emotions described: the love of parents, the grief that accompanies bereavement, the joy in offspring – these as well as jealousy, the envy, the malice of our human nature find place here. Separated by deep gulfs as they are from ourselves in many things, yet across the abysses we can clasp hands in a common humanity."[1]

Endnotes

1 Edwin W. Smith and Andrew Murray Dale, *The Ila-speaking Peoples and Northern Rhodesia*, Vol. 2. (New York: University Books, 1968), p. 345.

Chapter IX

TYPICAL LIFE CYCLE OF A VILLAGE BOY

To gain an insight into life cycle of a village boy in the district one needs to spend some time in and around the village. Fortunately, I lived by the side of Chief Choongo area, which was only a mile away from the Monze township.

Nogombe Fula's life cycle is very representative. He was born in a peasant family, and has three brothers and four sisters. He is healthy and jovial. His father sent him to a primary school in the village, aided and supported by the Zambian government. He used to get up at about six in the morning to take the family cattle to a grassy farm about half a mile from his village; at times his mother would ask him to get water from the well. By 7:30 a.m. he was ready to go to his elementary school which started at 8 a.m. By the time he had gone to begin his classes, he had helped the mother in bringing water for the family or in taking the cattle to the farm, or in helping the father in the backyard garden that produced beans, egg plants, and a small quantity of maize. Fula had already contributed his share of labor to the survival of his family. His father had only one wife.

Upon returning from school at 1 p.m., Fula, being the eldest issue in the family, took food along with all other members of the family. His brothers and sisters came to play with him after food, while parents would have a short but regular afternoon sleep. Since there was only one woman in the family, her control over the children was virtually supreme. Fula's father rebuked him in cases of hurting some one or playing too long into the evening. In the afternoon, he would go to collect the cattle. There was a football field and whenever a ball was available, the boys would play almost continuously until they were tired.

The boy's interest and activities varied depending on the season.

In the season of sowing maize, he was busy in the fields some distance from the house. In the rainy season he was expected to be called by the father to rise from bed early. In the evening, he sat by the side of the fire of cattle dung near the Kraal. His mother or at times his sisters brought thick inshima (porridge) together with a relish in the shape of some meat and gravy. He and his other relatives ate the porridge by breaking off the pieces and eating them after dipping in gravy. They were sometimes joined by one or two outsiders.

Newcomers and relatives occasionally came from different villages mostly for leisurely talks or for a plan to go to town next day for shopping. No newspapers or government bulletins came to the area. The sources of information were people and relatives coming from distant places. Talks among the family members and relatives included the possibility of marriage of a son or daughter, or sickness in the family. National politics and elections were of casual interests. At times family disputes were discussed.

After passing the grades in the primary school, Fula went to Monze Secondary School which had Forms 1 through 5, and the education was on the model of the British Ordinary Level G.C.E. The curriculum of the school included physics and chemistry among other subjects, taught by highly professional and dedicated expatriate teachers. These teachers came for a duration of three or more years and tried to impart knowledge to students as fast and thoroughly as possible. For the first time, Fula got his first impression of the outside world from the modern school environment and expatriate teachers. He soon became interested in science and did well also in these "modern" subjects. Though not brilliant, he managed to pass Form One with credit. Since the board and lodging were all free, he decided to stay in the school hostel, financed by the government. Here he found new friends and developed new ideas, and learned how to play tennis and badminton. He decided to be a teacher, a profession available to the graduates. After passing Form Three, he desired to go to Kabwe Teachers' Training School. Unfortunately he was not selected. He did not pass the Form Five Examination, organized by Overseas Cambridge Examination Board. As a drop out, he returned to his family in the village. He had no permanent employment in the village. He could not become a teacher; his education did not help him to cross the tribal economic boundary to the modern one. Frustration descended upon him. He remained a true follower of the community.

Nevertheless, he decided to improve his surroundings and use some of his ideas obtained from the Secondary School and from the foreign teachers. With his extra income from jobs with the expatriates at Monze, he built a family house, a well-constructed and nicely decorated hut. But all houses became infested with vermin. The old house got infested with the tick, a very unpleasant insect. Then the so-called jigger insect reached the house. He and his parents decided to move from that spot to a new one. Land was open and free.

As before, Fula would go to the field in the early morning, catch fish from the creek occasionally, and clear weeds in the house vegetable gardens. He decided to marry and the parents negotiated with the parents of a girl from Chief Monze's area. His wife became a part of the economic life in the new family, but the work remained monotonous and stagnant. Fula's education did not take him far into the modern economy, although many of his friends were lucky to be teachers. Some had gone to work in the copper mines in Ndola. Fula was raised in his village and remained in the village where things changed very slowly, if at all. Life was colorless and remained so.

APPENDIX I

Villages in Chief Monze's Area

1.	Beenzu	30.	Hachilala Hamunkeye
2.	Bulongo	31.	Hachilala
3.	Bbole	32.	Hachikena
4.	Chakatazya	33.	Hachuute
5.	Chalaba Mweene	34.	Hahuka
6.	Chaliyaba	35.	Hakansenke
7.	Cheelo	36.	Hamapende
8.	Cheelo Muchindu	37.	Hamazongo
9.	Chibozu	38.	Hamaavwa
10.	Chikwala	39.	Hamaluba
11.	Chikwangala	40.	Hamalau
12.	Chiwanga Maila	41.	Hamoonga
13.	Chiapula Diki	42.	Hamoonga Cheelo
14.	Chinjila	43.	Hamoonga Ngulube
15.	Chisowa	44.	Hamoonga Wankie
16.	Chiyasa	45.	Hamudebwe
17.	Chiyumu	46.	Hamukancali
18.	Chobana	47.	Hamungu
19.	Chumbu	48.	Hampende
20.	Chuube Chipongo	49.	Hanane
21.	Dabali	50.	Upuluka
22.	Domingo Jimba	51.	Hang'andu Hosea
23.	Dominic Nyimba	52.	Hang'andu Monze
24.	Gaali	53.	Hanguwa
25.	Habeenzu	54.	Hangila
26.	Hachiika	55.	Hataubile
27.	Hachiyabeka	56.	Hatabile Nzila
28.	Hachikandi	57.	Hatembo
29.	Hachikanga	58.	Hatontola

59. Hantebe Muleya	91. Makala
60. Hibbaba	92. Makulo Siamachila
61. Hilimi	93. Makondo
62. Himpande	94. Makwembo
63. Jempa Hanundwa	95. Makwempa
64. Jerico Edward	96. Malambo
65. Kabunda	97. Malambo Chinkuli
66. Kachengo	98. Malambo Timothy
67. Kachokola Siavwaala	99. Malama
68. Kagoli	100. Maupunu
69. Kanchele	101. Mandali
70. Kajamba	102. Matahataha
71. Kalulu	103. Masaka Shambwila
72. Kalimanzila	104. Michelo
73. Kangoni	105. Milimo
74. Kapapa Moomba	106. Miyanda Banji
75. Kasalala Namansenya	107. Miyanda
76. Kasalala Sikalapu	108. Miyanda Chidakwa
77. Kazemba	109. Miayanda Johane
78. Kazingwe	110. Miyanda Sypriano
79. Kazunga	111. Miyanda Robert
80. Lipeyo Manaumo	112. Miyoba
81. Liso	113. Mooba
82. Lubinga	114. Mooga Milimo
83. Lweendo	115. Monze
84. Lwiindi	116. Monze Bulanda
85. Maambo	117. Mondoma
86. Mabwizi	118. Mubila
87. Madonko	119. Muoololo
88. Mafuta	120. Mujahaliso
89. Maimbo	121. Mukapeka
90. Mainza	122. Mukamuchele

123.	Mulamba	155.	Nataala
124.	Mulindi	156.	Nydatamaluli
125.	Mulumbwa Mooya	157.	Nzala
126.	Mulangu	158.	Nzila
127.	Munamombe	159.	Ngoma
128.	Munankopa	160.	Nkandela
129.	Munakapongo	161.	Nyongani
130.	Mungoni	162.	Polomajole
131.	Munamuzongwe	163.	Punabantu
132.	Munamwala	164.	Saili Tonga
133.	Muunga	165.	Siabulombo
134.	Museete	166.	Siabumpindu
135.	Muzoka	167.	Siakaanga
136.	Mbozi	168.	Siakafwamba
137.	Mbozwa Mukoka	169.	Siampandula
138.	Mwaala	170.	Sianene
139.	Mwaalila	171.	Sianene Samson
140.	Mwampaule	172.	Sibitwane
141.	Mwanamalambo	173.	Sibusu
142.	Mwanamani	174.	Sichiimbwe
143.	Mwana Momba	175.	Sichiyanda
144.	Mwanamwanza	176.	Sichambwa Manasimbala
145.	Mwanankuku	177.	Sichimwe
146.	Mwangani	178.	Sichoonga
147.	Mweemba	179.	Sichoi
148.	Mweene	180.	Sichuwa
149.	Mweene Simavuma	181.	Sichubwa John
150.	Nacandwe	182.	Sihubwas Muuma
151.	Nalompota	183.	Sihubwa Samen
152.	Namanjele	184.	Sikabali
153.	Nampaka	185.	Sikalinda
154.	Namuwa	186.	Sikasiwa

187. Simanasa
188. Simoonga
189. Simoonga Sianguwa
190. Simoonga Milambo
191. Simoya
192. Simoya Eleot
193. Simupela
194. Simpela Ben
195. Simupobela
196. Simukale
197. Simuvwimi
198. Simweemba

199. Simukombwe
200. Simweendengwe
201. Simweete
202. Simweeleya
203. Simwiinga
204. Sinyendeende
205. Sinywimukandi
206. Sitima
207. Siauna
208. Tabele
209. Upakili

Villages in Chief Chona's Area

1. Chanwe
2. Cheele
3. Cheele Nabukuyu
4. Cheelo Singwima
5. Chibawa
6. Chilala
7. Chilumbwa
8. Chimweta
9. Chikuni
10. Chibona
11. Chona Chief
12. Chona Chobana
13. Habeenzu
14. Habeenzu Chuka
15. Hachanga
16. Halwiindi Chikuni

17. Halwiindi Dickson
18. Hamachonhe
19. Hamiya
20. Hamunyanga
21. Hakalaki
22. Hanyoola
23. Hanamonga
24. Kabimba
25. Kalombe Mulale
26. Kayumba
27. Kudumba
28. Lumamba
29. Mafule Moonga
30. Malambo
31. Malambo Job
32. Malengwe

33. Maambo Timothy
34. Mateketa
35. Miyoba Nakayuwa
36. Musende
37. Musende Simonga
38. Munankombo
39. Munankeya
40. Mutanti
41. Muzambalika
42. Mpokota
43. Mpokota Nchimunya

44. Mwenda
45. Mwiinga Chilala
46. Nalube
47. Naluube Mwanamambo
48. Namtaba
49. Saul Mutwa
50. Siasulwe
51. Sikabenga
52. Simuyanda
53. Wilson
54. Zanduka

Villages in Chief Choongo's Area

1. Beene
2. Cheepa Timothy
3. Cheepa Samson
4. Chibosha
5. Chilala Munyama
6. Chimpande
7. Chimpati
8. Chiingo
9. Chitanda
10. Choongo Mumba
11. Choobe
12. Choongo (Chief)
13. Chuchu
14. Chunka
15. Gwabi
16. Hatwiiko
17. Hamaluba

18. Kaizi Chiyoba
19. Kajamba
20. Kala
21. Kalindi Chingobe
22. Kaluwe
23. Kambeza
24. Kateya Cheepa
25. Macha
26. Maimbo
27. Makala
28. Makondo
29. Makuta
30. Malambo Sumangombe
31. Malumani Siamonda
32. Maambo Chinyama
33. Maambo Paul
34. Manyuchi

35. Mavumba Chikuni
36. Mbamunya
37. Menchela
38. Miyoba Reuben
39. Moombe
40. Moonga Peter
41. Mooya Ticky
42. Malambo Engles
43. Mukweeka
44. Mulomo Siamponge
45. Mumbuluma
46. Munachaandi
47. Munachuutwa Mungu
48. Mungaba Masenge
49. Munamazuba
50. Munyati
51. Munyati Haloma
52. Muponda
53. Mutamina
54. Muteze
55. Muyuwe
56. Mwanabimba Samson
    Beene
57. Maunzula
58. Mweete Sianyemu
59. Mwiinga Musongwa
60. Mwiinga Samson
61. Mpongo
62. Nakaoma
63. Nalipapa
64. Namalambo Malumani
65. Namangoma
66. Nawando
67. Nankambula
68. Ncheema
69. Nduuma Siamukobo
70. Ngandu
71. Ngandu Timothy
72. Ngombe
73. Siabasuna
74. Siabwani Jakopo
75. Siachibize
76. Siakulya
77. Sialwiindi
78. Siamakala
79. Siameno Michelo
80. Siamwiimbu
81. Sianayama
82. Siandiya Namajowe
83. Siangaila
84. Siangwele
85. Siankwandi
86. Sianzambwani
87. Siampakama
88. Siatila Jam
89. Siakwaambwa
90. Sichewo
91. Sichibabala
92. Simoonde Sikaumu
93. Simulowa
94. Zumbwe

Villages in Chief Mwanza's Area

1.	Bulimo	
2.	Bwanty	
3.	Cheelo Nagweluka	
4.	Joe	
5.	Chibinda Hakaungu	
6.	Chibozu	
7.	Chibbwalu	
8.	Chigabwa	
9.	Chikani	
10.	Chilapukila Chikaye	
11.	Chilemba	
12.	Chilonga Mweemba	
13.	Chinzila Amos	
14.	Chiyoma	
15.	Chisyoola	
16.	Chipembele	
17.	Chivumba	
18.	Chiyumba	
19.	Chizunga Siachibambo	
20.	Choobe Ndeleki	
21.	Choombwa	
22.	Chuuka Hamoonde	
23.	Habwizu Njombolo	
24.	Hagumba	
25.	Hakantu	
26.	Hakonze	
27.	Hamatako	
28.	Hamasanzu	
29.	Hamalyangombe	
30.	Hamayanda	

31. Hamoonga Ticky
32. Hamooy
33. Habanji
34. Hambulo
35. Hamwiinde
36. Handiya
37. Handome
38. Hatalimi
39. Hatukumbi
40. Hikapande
41. Kamwaye Miainga
42. Loonzola Jacob
43. Lweendo Cheelo
44. Machebe
45. Mainga Nabulwa
46. Makala
47. Makwembo
48. Makambo Simon
49. Malomo Phillip
50. Masowe
51. Mateyo
52. Michelo Patrol
53. Manumomba
54. Munamombe Chikamba
55. Mungolo
56. Muzyamba Isau
57. Mwanza (Chief)
58. Mwanwuonga
59. Mweemba Peter
60. Mweena Cheepa

61.	Mweena Nadongo	71.	Patuka Chingwela
62.	Mweene Njola	72.	Sikaambo
63.	Nachisakao	73.	Sikalozi
64.	Nalwiinga Mwete	74.	Sikaulu
65.	Namukamba	75.	Simankati
66.	Namulonya	76.	Simmonga
67.	Namwaze	77.	Simumba
68.	Nkaba Mwale	78.	Sintambo
69.	Nkabika	79.	Sintuba
70.	Ngandu Timothy	80.	Simwaalu

Villages in Chief Ufwenuka's Area

1.	Chilaba	19.	Hambala
2.	Chibozu	20.	Hampongo
3.	Chihibwa	21.	Hanamaila
4.	Chikonga Chibi	22.	Kang'ono Machisi
5.	Chinungwe	23.	Maohila
6.	Chimuka Amos	24.	Mainza Peter
7.	Chimuka Suntwe	25.	Makondo
8.	Chinyaka	26.	Maanya Ng'andu
9.	Chipembele	27.	Mawvili Cheelo
10.	Chisiwo Malambo	28.	Milambo
11.	Chizyato	29.	Milandu Haboya
12.	Chizyoli Miyanda	30.	Mukweclele
13.	Choobe Muganda	31.	Mulambe
14.	Haabumpimdu	32.	Mulinga
15.	Haachuumpa Mapulanga	33.	Munene
16.	Hakasondansima	34.	Muvwenga
17.	Hankumo	35.	Mbozi
18.	Hamakalu	36.	Mpande

37.	Mwaze	48.	Siampandula
38.	Mweemba	49.	Siamaamba
39.	Mwika Abraham	50.	Sikapade
41.	Mwiika Mwiinga	51.	Sikawaala Nzala
42.	Mwiinga Malawi	52.	Sikawaala Chihibwa
43.	Naluube	53.	Sikooma Mwiinga
44.	Nalusha	54.	Simoya
45.	Namakube	55.	Siaayi
46.	Nkombe	56.	Ufwenuka
47.	Nyimba		

Villages in Chief Siamusonde's Area

1.	Banji Davison	19.	Katazhaya
2.	Bwantu Sityole	20.	Kazolo
3.	Chibwate	21.	Kwalikumena
4.	Chibwanbwa	22.	Lubala
5.	Chikumbwe	23.	Lubemba
6.	Chilomo Enoch	24.	Lupabola
7.	Chinkuli	25.	Lusimbo
8.	Choke Nandaukila	26.	Machunka Soda
9.	Chuugwe	27.	Mainza
10.	Gwati	28.	Masinge
11.	Hachikoma	29.	Miyoba
12.	Hamagaba	30.	Mompo
13.	Hamaumbwe	31.	Mooya
14.	Hamusankwa	32.	Mugale
15.	Hamusonde	33.	Mulamba Simwze
16.	Himsongu	34.	Mulaya Nine
17.	Kaambwa	35.	Mulube Shibwanda
18.	Kashongo	36.	Munanomba

37.	Munang'andu	46.	Nalonda
38.	Muunta Makaaza	47.	Namakando Jim
39.	Muyangali Joshua	48.	Ng'andu
40.	Musoka Museka Tegula	49.	Ng'andu
41.	Mwanachigwele	50.	Sikapade
42.	Mwanakampwe	51.	Sikawaala Nzala
43.	Mwanamwami	52.	Sikawaala Chihibwa
44.	Mwanangonze	53.	Sikooma Mwiinga
45.	Mwangwe		

APPENDIX II

SONGS AND DANCES

Singing is often part of dancing. During a girl's or boy's initiation ceremony dancing is a must. In Monze area usually the following song is sung at a girl's initiation ceremony. The parents come forward to express their happiness while receiving so many visitors. These relatives and outsiders have come to rejoice with the parents because their child is now a "mature" person. Parents are excited and as such they sing:

> Ndasekelale.
> > Beenzu bangu
> > Beenzu bangu
> > Boonse aaba.
> > Beenzu bangu
> > Beenzu bangu ndiindi.

When translated from Tonga to English the song means:

> > I am proud to welcome my visitors.
> > Oh, my visitors.
> > All these are my visitors,
> > yes, my visitors certainly.

BIBLIOGRAPHY

Allan, William. "African Land Usage," *Rhodes-Livingstone Journal*, No. 2 (June 1945).

Anthony, Kenneth R.M., and Victor C. Uchenda. *Agricultural Change in the Mazabuka District*. Stanford: Food Research Institute, 1960.

Atlas for Zambia. Glasgow: William Collins Sons, 1973.

Barber, William J. *The Economy of British Central Africa*. Stanford: Stanford University Press, 1961.

Barnes, James A. *A Politics in a Changing Society*. London: 1897.

Bates, Robert H. *Rural Responses to Industrialization*. New Haven: Yale University Press, 1976.

Bloom, L. "Some Values and Attitudes of Young Zambia, Studies Through Spontaneous Autobiographies," *African Social Research* [Lusaka], No. 14, (December 1972), 288–300.

Brelsford, W.V. *The Tribes of Northern Rhodesia*. Lusaka: Government Printer, 1957.

Chibesakunda, Lombe. "The Rights of Divorcees Under Statutory Law," in *Report of Consultation on Women's Rights in Zambia, Women in Zambia*. Kitwe: Mindolo Ecumenical Centre, 1970 (mimeo).

_____. "The Rights of Married Women under Statutory Law," in *Report of Consultuation on Women's Rights in Zambia, Women in Zambia*. Kitwe: Mindolo Ecumenical Centre, 1970 (mimeo).

____. "The Rights of Widows under Statutory Law," in *Report of Consultation on Women's Rights in Zambia, Women in Zambia*. Kitwe: Mindolo Ecumenical Center, 1970 (mimeo).

Clark, J.D. *The Prehistory of Africa*. New York: Praeger, 1970.

Colson, Elizabeth. *Marriage and Family Among the Tonga of Northern Rhodesia*. Manchester, 1958.

____. *Social Organization of the Gwembe Tonga*. Manchester: Manchester University Press, 1960.

____. *The Plateau Tonga of Northern Rhodesia: Social and Religious Studies*. Manchester: Manchester University Press; New York: Humanities Press, 1962.

Colson, Elizabeth, and Max Gluckman. *Seven Tribes of Central Africa*. London: Oxford University Press, 1967.

Colson, Elizabeth, and T. Scudder. "New Economic Relationships between the Gwembe Valley and the Line of Rail," 190–212 in David Parkin (ed.), *Town in Country in Central and Eastern Africa*. London: Oxford University Press for International African Institute, 1975.

Coupland, Sir Reginald. *Livingstone's Last Journey*. London: Collins, 1945; New York: Macmillan, 1947.

Dresang, Eliza T. *The Land and People of Zambia*. Philadelphia: Lippincott, 1975.

Fagan, Brian M., et al. *Iron Age Culture in Zambia*. 2 vols. London: Chatto and Windus, 1967, 1969.

Fagan, Brian M. (ed.) *A Short History of Zambia from the Earliest Times until A.D. 1900*. London: Oxford University Press, 1966 (reprinted with revision, 1968).

____. "Zambia and Rhodesia," 215–244 in P.L. Shinnie, *The African Iron Age*. London: Oxford University Press, 1971.

Gann, Lewis H. *The Birth of a Plural Society: The Development of Northern Rhodesia Under the British South Africa Company*. Manchester: Manchester University Press, 1958.

____. *A History of Northern Rhodesia*. London: Chatto & Windus, 1964.

____. *Zambia*. New York: Praeger, 1965.

Gluckman, Max, and Colson, Elizabeth. *Seven Tribes of British Central Africa*. Manchester: Manchester University Press, 1959.

Hall, Richard. *Zambia*. New York: Fredrick A Praeger, 1967.

Hellen, John A. *Rural Economic Development in Zambia, 1890–1964*. New York: Humanities Press, 1968.

Jones, A.D. "Social Networks of Farmers Among the Plateau Tonga of Zambia," in P.C. Lloyd, ed., *The New Elites of Tropical Africa*. Oxford: Oxford Univesity Press, 1966.

Kaplan, Irving. *Zambia: A Country Study.* Washington D.C.: The American University, 1979.

Kaplan, Irving, et al. *Area Handbook for Zambia.* (2d ed., DA Pam 550–75). Washington: GPO for Foreign Area Studies, The American University, 1974.

Kaunda, Kenneth. *Zambia Shall Be Free.* London: Heinemann, 1962; New York: Praeger, 1963.

Kay, George. *A Social History of Zambia.* London: Universty of London Press, 1967.

Livingstone, David. *The Last Journals of David Livingstone.* London: John Murray, 1874; New York: Harper, 1875.

_____. *Livingstone's Private Journals.* ed. Isaac Schapera. London: Chatto & Windus; Berkeley: University of California Press, 1960.

Lloyd P.C., ed. *The New Elites of Tropical Africa.* Oxford: Oxford University Press, 1966.

Mackintosh, C.W. *Coillard of the Zambesi.* London: Unwin, 1907.

Nchete, Fr. Dominic. *History of Monze Chief.* Typescript, 1975.

Ottenberg, Simon and Phoebe. *Cultures and Societies in Africa.* New York: Random House, 1960.

Richards, Audrey I. *Land, Labour and Diet in Northern Rhodesia.* London: Oxford University Press, 1939.

Roberts, Andrew D. *A History of Zambia.* New York: African Pubishing, 1976.

Rotberg, Robert I. *Christian Missionaries and the Creation of Northern Rhodesia, 1880–1924.* Princeton: Princeton University Press, 1965.

____. *The Rise of Nationalism in Central Africa: The Making of Malawi and Zambia, 1873–1964.* Cambridge: Harvard University Press, 1965.

Service, Elan R. *Primitive Social Organization: An Evolutionary Perspective.* New York, Random House, 1962.

Smith, Edwin W., and Dale, Andrew Murray. *The Ila-Speaking People of Northern Rhodesia*, Vol. 2. London: Macmillan, 1920.

Southall, William A. *Social Change in Modern Africa.* Oxford: Oxford University Press, 1969.

Thomson, J.B. *Joseph Thomson, African Explorer.* London: Sampson Low, 1896.

Tindall, P.E.N. *A History of Central Africa.* New York: Praeger, 1968.

Wallis, J.P.R. ed. *The Zambezi Expedition of David Livingstone.* London: Chatto and Windus, 1956.

Willis, A.J. *An Introduction to the History of Central Africa.* London: Oxford University Press, 1985.

Young, C., and Banda, Hastings Kamuzu (ed.). *Our African Way of Life*. London: Butterworth, 1964.

Unpublished Sources

Father Dominic Nchete – Livingstone Museum Papers.
Father Moreau. *A History of Chikuni Mission* (1975).
Personal Records of Chief Chona (District Boma Headquarters).
Personal Records of Chief Choongo (District Boma Headquarters).
Personal Records of Chief Monze (District Boma Headquarters).
Personal Records of Chief Mwanza (District Boma Headquarters).
Personal Records of Chief Siamasonde (District Boma Headquarters).

INDEX

African National Congress
(ANC) 20, 28, 29, 44

Barotseland 2, 3, 15, 16, 31, 52

Bemba 3, 12, 13, 19, 51

British South Africa (BSA)
Company 4, 16, 26, 40, 52–54, 67

Catechists' Training Centre
60, 65, 66

Central African Federation 6, 19, 29

Chief Benjamin Bbandika 30

Chief Chona 14, 15, 23, 25, 28, 40, 47, 77, 96, 108

Chief Choongo 14, 23, 24, 25, 29, 30, 31–36, 98, 101

Chief Choongo Hamanchenga
30, 35

Chief Haamajani 27

Chief Haameja 43

Chief Haameja Chona 43, 45

Chief Haamiyanda Nchete 26

Chief Japhet Chidamba 36, 37

Chief Longwani Mweemba 27, 28

Chief Monze 7, 12–16, 19, 23, 25–27, 29, 32, 52, 57, 81, 95, 103

Chief Monze Nchete 26, 27

Chief Munakembe 30, 31, 35

Chief Mutonga 25

Chief Mwanachingwala 28

Chief Mwanampongwe 30, 35

Chief Mwanza 14, 23, 24, 25, 32, 36, 37, 42, 43, 68, 69, 82

Chief Mweemba 27

Chief Siamusonde 14, 23, 24, 25, 28, 32, 38, 39

Chief Simon Mumba 45

Chief Ufwenuka 23, 24, 25, 28, 32, 33, 39, 40, 81, 83, 97

Chikuni 17, 24–26, 40, 43, 45, 51, 54, 55–59, 66, 91

Chikuni Mission 56

Chisekesi 26, 91

Chona, Mainza 19, 20, 43–45

Chona, Mark 43, 45

Colson, Elizabeth 1, 5, 7, 79, 83

Copper 6, 13, 16, 103

Copperbelt 5, 18

Corboy, Bishop James 17, 61

Coryndon, R.T. 16, 52, 54

District Commissioner (DC)
27, 28, 29, 30, 36, 46, 57, 74, 75

District Secretary (DS) 34, 71-73, 75, 91

Gwembe 14, 15, 41, 79

Hut-tax 16

Ivory 2, 13, 15, 16

Kabwe 4, 103

Kafue 2, 14-16, 59
　　River 2, 12, 14

Kalomo 1, 4, 26, 52, 53, 55, 59

Kapapa, Cletus 28, 29

Kapwepwe, Simon 19

Kaunda, Kenneth David 6,
　　18, 19, 20, 44, 45, 73, 89

Lake Kariba 1, 6

Livingstone City 11, 17, 20,
　　43, 59, 63

Livingstone, David 3, 7, 16,
　　25, 38, 51–53

Lochinvar 2, 14, 15, 19

Lozi 2, 11, 12, 15, 16, 37, 38,
　　40, 41, 42, 51

Lusaka 4, 14, 17, 20, 43, 44,
　　61, 63, 65, 77

Lwangwa 1, 6

Magoye 1, 14, 58

Maize 4, 5, 15, 17–20, 34, 35,
　　40, 80, 81, 87, 90, 92, 101,
　　102

Malawi 3, 34, 63, 64, 66

Mazabuka 1, 4, 5, 15, 16, 19,
　　28, 36, 46
　　Boma 4, 16, 57
　　District
　　　　Commissioner 4, 65

Mongonti, R. Hamalambo 28

Monomotapa 13

Monze 1, 2, 4–7, 12, 13,
　　15–20, 23, 25, 26, 27, 29,
　　30, 36, 43, 45, 51, 52, 54,
　　60, 66, 71, 74, 76, 80, 91,
　　103
　　administration 89
　　Boma 16, 29, 71
　　Catholic 17, 54
　　chiefdom 7
　　Courts 78, 80, 82,
　　　　84
　　Diocese 66, 68
　　European farming
　　　　5
　　farmers 5, 6, 90
　　Fort 16
　　Hospital 17
　　Markets 75, 87
　　Police 77
　　Rural Council 17
　　settlers 90
　　township 90, 91,
　　　　101
　　Township Council
　　　　17

Monze Government Primary
　　School 7

Monze Night School 96

Monze Secondary School 7, 17,
　　18, 60, 68, 80, 91, 102– 103

Musekesi 17

Nampeyo 19, 20, 23, 25, 41–43, 45

Namwala 19, 30, 31, 59

Ndebele 11, 16, 37, 40

Ngoni 1, 16

Njola 24, 25, 36, 37, 68, 69, 112

Nkumbula, Harry 6, 19, 44

Nyanja 13

Patel 18, 28, 91

Plateau Tonga 5, 79

Plateau Tonga Native Authority 28, 46, 74, 75

Portuguese 2, 3, 7, 12, 13

Rhodes, Cecil 3, 26, 52, 53, 54

Rusangu 67, 68

Rusangu Secondary School 17, 60

Seventh Day Adventist (SDA) Church 53, 67, 68

Seventh-Day Adventist (SDA) Church 67

Seventh-Day Adventist Church 51

Slaves 2

Tagore Primary School 7, 18

Tonga 1, 2, 5, 7, 12, 13, 15, 26, 37, 46, 52, 58, 79, 80

   characteristic features 2

family 79, 88, 89, 91, 92

farmers 87, 92

marriage and divorce 83

settlements 2

sites 1, 2

tradition 95

villages 2

United National Independence Party (UNIP) 6, 18, 20, 44

Victoria Falls 4, 6

Village Registration and Development Act 73

Zambezi River 1, 3, 5, 13, 15, 18, 26, 30, 36, 51, 52

Zambia 1–8, 12, 18, 19, 44, 46, 51, 75, 76, 87

   Courts 77

   family 90

   marriage and divorce 85

   settlement 2

   slave trade 2

   tribal life 7

Zambia African National Congress (ZANC) 44

Zambia College of Agriculture 17, 60

Zambian National Assembly 73